9673

D0467290

PRAISE FOR
THE WORSHIP GOD
IS SEEKING

When David Ruis speaks, his words are some of the most challenging and inspiring I have heard. This book is no different. It is full of biblical and personal insights into the true meaning of worship, containing a timely and powerful message for God's people.

Tim Hughes

Author, *Here I Am to Worship*
Worship Leader and Songwriter

David Ruis has produced another great work—sans melody. It's as if while David was writing *The Worship God Is Seeking,* God was whispering in his ear. Written with pointed clarity and convicting, convincing biblical truth, this book reminds me of the faithful and passionate mercies of God and to "embrace Him as my sole source of life and love."

Kate Miner

Singer, *Live from the Sunset Strip*
Mom and Writer

When you usher in the King in worship, you also usher in His kingdom. You can't split up the two— if we're proclaiming the rule and reign of Jesus, then we'll expect to see aspects of that rule and reign exploding all over the place. David Ruis gets right to the heart of this in an excellent and original book. Filled with dramatic journeys through Scripture and powerful examples from his own life experiences, David encourages us to view this world, and our lives of worship, through the lens of the kingdom of God. *The Worship God Is Seeking* is a powerful invitation to Kingdom-based worship, and an urgent summons to Kingdom-infused living.

Matt Redman

Author, *Facedown* and *The Unquenchable Worshipper*
Worship Leader

THE
WORSHIP
GOD
IS SEEKING

DAVID RUIS

Regal

From Gospel Light
Ventura, California, U.S.A.

Regal

PUBLISHED BY REGAL BOOKS
FROM GOSPEL LIGHT
VENTURA, CALIFORNIA, U.S.A.
PRINTED IN THE U.S.A.

Regal Books is a ministry of Gospel Light, a Christian publisher
dedicated to serving the local church. We believe God's vision
for Gospel Light is to provide church leaders with biblical, user-friendly
materials that will help them evangelize, disciple and minister
to children, youth and families.

It is our prayer that this Regal book will help you discover
biblical truth for your own life and help you meet the needs
of others. May God richly bless you.

*For a free catalog of resources from Regal Books/Gospel Light, please call
your Christian supplier or contact us at* 1-800-4-GOSPEL
or www.regalbooks.com.

Rights for publishing this book in other languages are
contracted by Gospel Light Worldwide, the international nonprofit
ministry of Gospel Light. Gospel Light Worldwide also provides
publishing and technical assistance to international publishers
dedicated to producing Sunday School and Vacation Bible School
curricula and books in the languages of the world. For additional
information, visit www.gospellightworldwide.org; write to Gospel Light
Worldwide, P.O. Box 3875, Ventura, CA 93006; or send an e-mail
to info@gospellightworldwide.org.

Cover design by David Griffing

Library of Congress Cataloging-in-Publication Data
Ruis, David.
 The worship God is seeking / David Ruis.
   p. cm.
 ISBN 0-8307-3692-1 (hardcover)
 1. Public worship. 2. God—Worship and love. I. Title.

BV15.R85 2005
264—dc22   2005000128

1 2 3 4 5 6 7 8 9 10 / 10 09 08 07 06 05

DEDICATION

Anita, *my truest friend and ally—you have taken me to places along life's journey that I would have missed without your insight and love. You make me a better worshipper.*

My children:

Tamara, *you have caused me to reflect and go deeper many times. Thank you, my daughter.* Crystal, *you see into life in a very special way. Thank you for the many questions—keep asking.* Jael, *your love of life and willingness to try anything are an inspiration to me—don't ever stop.* Josiah, *your laughter and rhythm give me hope for the future. Thanks, son—keep leading on.*

CONTENTS

ACKNOWLEDGMENTS

I am so grateful for my parents, Jack and Alice, and my sister, Sandi. Thanks for helping mold me into who I am today, and impacting so much of how I see the world and its Creator.

Thanks to the Regal team, especially to Deena Davis, for rolling with so many twists and turns in the production of the manuscript. Your willingness to work with me and your insights along the way were indispensable in the final product.

I must say a very special thanks to Don Williams, a true friend and mentor. Don, you are an anchor in the swirl of my world, and your encouragement has been strength to me. Thanks so much, and a very deep thanks to Tap as well, for letting me invade your space so much. Much love to you both!

Deep thanks to Sheri McConnell. You have been such a gift to my whole family, and your support and friendship mean the world to all of us. Here's to many more years of partnership.

Finally, I must acknowledge the many friends and people who have walked in community with us through our adventures in Kelowna, Kansas City,

Winnipeg, and now, Los Angeles. In mentioning just a few of you, I am saying thanks to you all. I would not be where I am today without you. Thanks to Jan and Coral, Colin and Cynthia, the Rademakers, Marc Pusch, Brian and Shannon, Nathan and Kendra, Harv and Sue, the leadership team of WCV, Noel and Dona and the whole Himalayan Vineyard family, Doug and Rachel, Mike and Diane, JOEY, Kenny, Randy, Charles, Chris and Jennifer, Jamie and Pam, Colby, the Wiebes, the Trasks, the Janzens, the Heaslips, Sean and Christy, the NewLife team, the ministerial in Tujunga, Gary and Brenda, the Bests, VMG and the international Association of Vineyard Churches.

Chapter One

An **INVITATION** to **THE** **JOURNEY**

From time to time the church should take stock of that which is most central, most important and most vital in our common life together. Though we sing with the tongues of men and of angels, if we are not truly worshipping the living God, we are noisy gongs and clanging cymbals. Though we organize the liturgy most beautifully, if it does not enable us to worship the living God, we are mere ballet dancers. Though we repave the floor and reface the stonework, though we balance our budgets and attract all the tourists, if we are not worshipping God, we are nothing.

—N. T. WRIGHT, *FOR ALL GOD'S WORTH: TRUE WORSHIP AND THE CALLING OF THE CHURCH*

It's time again—time to rediscover the worship that has God at its center. If He's not at the heart of our gathering together, then what is our liturgy all about? The last thing we all need is just another meeting— God included. Just as He was longing for something beyond sacrifice and burnt offerings in times past, God's desire today is for worship that is centered more on relationship than liturgy. As we draw near to God, He draws near to us (see Jas. 4:8). Reclaiming the trust that was lost in Eden is at the heart of this encounter.

> Therefore, when Christ came into the world, He said: "Sacrifices and offerings, burnt offerings and sin offerings you did not desire, nor were you pleased with them" (although the law required them to be made). Then he said, "Here I am, I have come to do your will" (Heb. 10:5,8-9).

The worship God seeks relies completely on His initiative, knowing that the only true expression of worship is through the abandonment of all our agendas for His, as we trust in His sovereign power and unlimited grace. It is from this heart posture that true liturgy flows, that music and the arts find their highest calling and that the light of a worshipping community shines as a beacon of hope to a suffering and searching world.

GOD AT THE CENTER

Impacted by a global culture of consumerism, ever-changing technology and postmodern angst, it can be difficult for us to become part of anything that does not exist for our benefit. We are hesitant to

The journey into worship is a lifelong pursuit of discovering God in His Word and seeing Him constantly at work in our everyday lives and the world around us.

embrace anything that inconveniences or challenges our personal opinions and comfort, and so abandoned worship can appear ridiculous. Yet at the core of true worship is a life that gives up everything. It's not about what's in it for "us"; rather, it's about being broken and humbled before the King of eternity as we lay down our lives and agendas before Him.

Do we *know* God? Are we willing to wrestle with what it means to live under His kingdom reign? As we seek to cultivate the worship God seeks, theology (knowledge of God and His ways) is essential. Our worship needs to be anchored to the unalterable and eternal truths of who He is and the impact of His advancing kingdom on the earth. The journey into worship is a lifelong pursuit of discovering God in His Word and seeing Him constantly at work in our everyday lives and the world around us.

Without our realizing it, worship can become a commodity, or used as a means to an end. This creates an ever-increasing pressure within the local church to see worship as something to be used for many different purposes: a church growth tool; an evangelistic device; an atmosphere setter; a warm-up for the preaching of the Word; a source of income through publishing and recording; and the list goes on.

It would seem that we are at risk of creating a church culture in which aesthetics and entertainment become the watermark for a great worship experience. We are constantly evaluating the effectiveness of worship by the response of people. We paint a picture of God as a Being who is there for our benefit, and we "view worship as designed to reinforce our basic selfishness, masked under 'meeting our needs.'"[1]

HOW WE PERCEIVE WORSHIP

Several things within Christian subculture contribute to our attitudes toward worship. The emerging popularity of worship music and the resulting influence of worship leaders/artists, songwriters and worship bands have had a definite impact. Ten or fifteen years ago it was unheard of that a worship leader and/or songwriter would have an opportunity to make a living outside of vocational church ministry. Today, the explosion of publishing royalties and the popularity of worship artists who have gained almost rock-star status have brought worship to the forefront of the Christian music industry. Worship music has emerged into its own genre. While this growth is exciting on the one hand, and a sign of health for the Church as she steps into her role as a worshipping community, it is a path through a mine field of money, fame, and all the dynamics that these bring.

When I wrote some of my earliest compositions for church usage, I never once thought that this would become a way to earn a living. Songs outside of the hymnal and a few worn-out "Jesus People" choruses were very scarce. Songwriting in the local church was simply the result of being in a community desperate to find fresh expressions of worship. I find it a struggle to maintain that kind of innocence today, as I write songs that are introduced into an already glutted marketplace and see recordings lost in the swirl of distribution deals and demographics.

It is critical that we pause long enough to see where we are. Whom are we really doing this for? Is God even listening? There are no easy answers here, but definitely we must have courage to ask the hard questions and fight for a simplicity and devotion at the heart of our worship expression.

Another dynamic within current culture that influences our approach to worship is the desire to make our worship accessible to people who are seeking after God yet may be unfamiliar with our particular liturgy or church culture. It is critical that we create bridges of understanding for people who may discover God through a church meeting; but it is just as important that we maintain a God-centered focus in worship. There is nothing worse than someone's journey toward God being frustrated by unnecessary Christian clichés and religious baggage.

However, we must not be ashamed of worship that is biblically authentic, or become insecure living in a society that has the potential of being hostile toward God and His ways. He is our King, and we should not fear "those who kill the body and after that can do no more"; rather, we fear Him who "after the killing of the body, has power to throw you into hell" (Luke 12:4-5).

God is the focus of true worship. This truth has inherent challenges that no amount of tweaking and adjusting can ease.

> For we are to God the aroma of Christ among those who are being saved and those who are perishing. To the one we are the smell of death; to the other, the fragrance of life. And who is equal to such a task? (1 Cor. 2:15-16).

It's All About God

The fact is, worship is an end in itself. It is for God. To lose sight of Him is to lose sight of worship altogether. All begins and ends with Him.

The stance is not passive, however. This kind of worship is engaged. Over and over in the book of Revelation we see the elders throwing down their crowns, bowing low before their God (see Rev. 4:9-11). The original language is clear. It is voluntary. This is not a reaction to being overwhelmed by His glory or overcome by something external. The elders are moved by the revelation of who it is they stand before, and by a deliberate act of the will they bow.

> You are worthy, our Lord and God, to receive glory and honor and power, for you created all things, and by your will they were created and have their being (Rev. 4:11).

The resulting power of this kind of worship shifts the focus from the worshippers to the One being worshipped. The attention shifts from the worship team, the choir, the liturgist and the preacher to the Lord. No longer is worship about performance and presentation. God is present. This posture is deliberate, not waiting for a mystical presence but stepping into the reality of who God is. No longer is worship simply about receiving a touch and getting goose bumps. God is here, and His kingdom has come.

It is in this place that God reveals Himself as He chooses to descend and dwell with His Church. This is the biblical understanding of worship. Even though

God dwells in the courts of heaven with angels and living creatures in attendance, He condescends to inhabit the praise of his people[2] (see Ps. 22:3); Jesus is found in the midst of the congregation singing to the Father (see Heb. 2:12); and as we draw near to God, He draws near to us (see Jas. 4:8). The Holy Spirit, proceeding from the Father and the Son, has freedom here to glorify Christ, establishing righteousness, judgment and justice, empowering the Church to do His work.

As God draws near, so the fullness of His Triune presence and His kingdom come. To invite God's presence is to invite His kingdom reign. All agendas must be laid aside for His. All other authorities and powers must submit to Him or face the consequences. There is no room for idols. All that is false will be exposed. The true worship experience is not a liturgy devoid of power and life-changing implications. The King is here, and His kingdom has come.

At times we may be uncomfortable with this kind of worship encounter. The worship that focuses on God first, acknowledging His presence among us, can be unsettling. We are not welcoming a force to empower us, nor invoking the presence of a distant deity. This is not about aligning ourselves with good ideas or philosophizing about the concept of God. It is about acknowledging that He is real. He is alive. God has thoughts, opinions, feelings and insight about what is happening among us. Just as we see Jesus strolling through the churches in Revelation, evaluating what He observed, so, too, He interacts with us in the Church today, wanting to be fully included in the life of our community and fellowshiping with us (see Rev. 3:20). Amazing!

So, then, making way for God in our worship is not something vague or theoretical. What makes worship truly Christian is its proximity. God is in the room. Worship is now not only objective, it is also deeply personal. Songs are no longer just *about* God, they are sung *to* God. Displays of adoration are not inappropriate but are a vital part of the worship's authenticity. Worship becomes about responding to God's presence. The dynamics of the liturgy change from that of a monologue to a dialogue and response as the present rule and reign of heaven break through. God is here, and we will never be the same.

Most church meetings are for worship, the sacraments and the proclamation of God's Word—all three of which, incidentally, may lead to healing and other works of God.[3]

The presence of God is no longer out of reach; the Kingdom is here and manifest amongst us.

RECLAIMING THE TREASURE

A. W. Tozer once observed that worship was "the missing jewel of the church."[4] Worship is something to be treasured, held with the awareness that it is not ours to keep. Lucifer would have done well to heed this advice. Worship is not about us. It is with a sweet mix of sobriety and inexpressible joy that we enter in, knowing that we are engaging in something divine that is not inspired by human ingenuity or empty religiosity. It is a work of grace. We are drawn to participate in something that is beyond our own efforts.

> As the deer pants for streams of water, so my soul pants for you, O God. My soul thirsts for God, for the living God. When can I go and meet with God? (Ps. 42:1-2).

> My soul yearns, even faints, for the courts of the LORD; my heart and my flesh cry out for the living God (Ps. 84:2).

The invitation is clear. We do not forsake gathering together, as is the habit of some, but we run to the place of worship to meet with God Himself. The worship that God seeks is not out of our reach. We can journey here together and in this place of complete abandonment and trust touch the face of God and satisfy the deepest longings of our souls.

From time to time the Church should take stock of that which is most central, most important and most vital in our common life together. Now is the time. Let's discover the worship He is longing for.

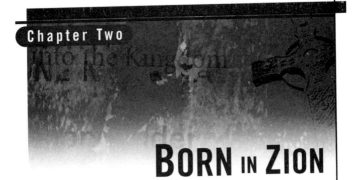

Chapter Two

BORN IN ZION

*What is the purpose of Yahweh seated
upon his throne, dwelling in his heavenly
palace with his angelic court and his earthly
subjects gathered before him? The answer
can be given in a word: worship.*

—DON WILLIAMS, *SIGNS AND WONDERS
AND THE KINGDOM OF GOD*

One of the most consistent biblical images we have of God is of Him on His throne. From the pages of the Old Testament to the Revelation of John, we see God enthroned. To see God is to see Him as King.

The throne from which God rules is in Zion; the place of unending worship. It is here that God delights to dwell. His throne is the praises of His people (see Ps. 22:3), and the place He delights to be is where His people gather to praise Him.

He has set his foundation on the holy mountain; the LORD loves the gates of Zion more than all the dwellings of Jacob. Glorious things are said of you, O city of God: "I will record Rahab and Babylon among those who acknowledge me—Philistia too, and Tyre, along with Cush—and will say, 'This one was born in Zion.'" Indeed, of Zion it will be said, "This one and that one were born in her, and the Most High himself will establish her." The LORD will write in the register of the peoples: "This one was born in Zion." As they make music they will sing, "All my fountains are in you" (Ps. 87).

The sons of Korah wrote this ancient song to accompany them as they tended the doors of the Temple in Jerusalem. Many say that it was written at the founding of David's city of Zion,[1] Jerusalem. Though its melody is lost to us, it continues to point us toward the beauty and mystery of the eternal Zion, the place of worship where

> His kingdom will have its center (Mic. 4:8) in vindication (Isa. 62:1,11) and in joy (61:3). The God of Zion will, moreover, reign forever (Ps. 146:10; Mic. 4:7), in His city, which will never be removed (Isa. 33:20). Zion has here received its final association with that ultimate kingdom of God's new heaven and new earth . . . and its glory marks the termination of history's whole present cycle of sun and moon, day and night (Isa. 33:23; cf. Rev. 20:11-21; 5; 22:5).[2]

GOD RULES

Our acknowledgment of God does not make Him who He is. It is not our worship that establishes His rule, for His government is from everlasting to everlasting and His kingdom will never end. He is not a president who is voted into power via a democratic process. He is not a prime minister acting on behalf of some heavenly parliament, nor is He a CEO. God does not rule as a dictator, usurping authority and maintaining power through a reign of terror. No. He is King.

So, too, we see the reign of Jesus as complete and unchallenged. "On his robe and on his thigh he has this name written: KING OF KINGS AND LORD OF LORDS" (Rev. 19:16). All of human history is moving toward one climactic moment when at the name of Jesus every knee will bow "in heaven and on earth and under the earth, and every tongue confess that Jesus Christ is Lord, to the glory of God the Father" (Phil. 2:10-11).

Before all is said and done, there will be no living thing that will not openly acknowledge the kingship of Jesus. Not one person, not one angel, not one demon will escape the call to bow and confess Him as Lord. For those who will not acknowledge Christ before the final judgment, this will be terrifying. There will be kings, princes, generals, the rich, the mighty, slaves and free people—all will call for the mountains to fall on them rather than face the Lamb. But they will bow. They will confess, even though salvation is no longer within their reach (see Rev. 6:16-17). Satan himself, cringing and shrieking, will proclaim in front of the nations of the earth with all creation watching, "Jesus is Lord!"

The Father and the Son are in complete unity, reigning over nature, history, kings and kingdoms.

Why do the nations conspire and the peoples plot in vain? The kings of the earth take their stand and the rulers gather together against the LORD and against his Anointed One. "Let us break their chains," they say, "and throw off their fetters." The One enthroned in heaven laughs; the Lord scoffs at them. Then he rebukes them in his anger and terrifies them in his wrath, saying, "I have installed my King on Zion, my holy hill." I will proclaim the decree of the LORD: He said to me, "You are my Son; today I have become your Father. Ask of me, and I will make the nations your inheritance, the ends of the earth your possession. You will rule them with an iron scepter; you will dash them to pieces like pottery." Therefore, you kings, be wise; be warned, you rulers of the earth. Serve the LORD with fear and rejoice with trembling. Kiss the Son, lest he be angry and you be destroyed in your way, for his wrath can flare up in a moment. Blessed are all who take refuge in him (Ps. 2).

Here is where it all begins and ends, on our faces before the King of heaven. He initiates worship, and He is the sole focus of it. All is for God. He is King. To live under His kingdom rule is to become a worshipper, to turn and kiss the Son.

GOD DESIRES TRUE, COVENANT RELATIONSHIP WITH US

While God is rightful ruler of all, and His foundation secure and unshakable—even the demons understand God's rule and tremble at His Word (see Jas. 2:19)—He seeks something more. He doesn't want just a King and vassal relationship. In addition to being seen as the dominant ruler over all other deities or gods of this age, He longs for true and deep covenant.

This is what the LORD says: "Heaven is my throne, and the earth is my footstool. Where is the house you will build for me? Where will my resting place be?" (Isa. 66:1).

Day of Atonement

Though He desires to take up His dwelling amongst us, His holiness is incompatible with the unredeemed human condition. The human being—body, soul and spirit—damaged by sin, cannot easily survive an encounter in this place of unveiled worship. The experience is so intense that during the days before the coming of Christ, there was only one person, from one nation, in one place who could enter the most holy place at the heart of Zion. Even this privileged priest could enter only one time a year—and this was entirely by God's initiation and invitation. Strict protocol had to be adhered to on this special day known as the Day of Atonement, or the life of the high priest would be forfeit.

This Day of Atoning was a deeply moving and powerful event in the Jewish calendar that spoke of God's desire to dwell among the people He had created. The Day spoke of His mercy and concern regarding the barrier that the sin of the nation created between God and His people. Yet this observance of blood sacrifice and its ceremony could only do so much, and it would have to be repeated year after year.

Who can ascend this hill of the Lord (see Ps. 24:3)? Who can reach this place of Zion? No one. There is no one with a heart pure enough, not one with clean hands. There is none righteous—no, not one.

The Redeemer
Yet look again.

> Lift up your heads, O you gates; be lifted up, you ancient doors, that the King of glory may come in. Who is this King of glory? The LORD strong and mighty, the LORD mighty in battle. Lift up your heads, O you gates; lift them up, you ancient doors, that the King of glory may come in. Who is he, this King of glory? The LORD Almighty—he is the King of glory (Ps. 24:7-10).

There is One who comes to make a way for all the rest. He comes clothed in the robes of humanity with nothing in His appearance that should attract us to Him (see Isa. 53:2). He comes in compassion to be the servant of all. He comes as a Man of Sorrows, familiar with suffering (see Isa. 53:3). But do not be fooled. There is much power here. Stand aside, for He comes to destroy the works of the devil and to shatter the bonds of iniquity that hold us all. His battle cry is one of mercy and His arsenal filled with the weapons of love. This is the Lord, mighty in battle—this is the King of glory.

There can be no ascension to the place of worship for any person without outside help, and so God descends to liberate His people. Just as God came down to deliver the Israelites from the hands of the Egyptians, Jesus steps down from His throne to liberate us from the works of Satan through His death on the cross and resurrection to His rightful place of rule at God's right hand. Just as God led His children into the land of promise and established a nation, so we see Jesus as the head of the Church, the firstborn over all creation, establishing and building a Church whose members are under His kingdom rule. Just as praise awaits God in Zion, so Jesus will win His Bride from the four corners of the earth to rule with Him and worship forever.

A lasting atonement needed to be made, and there was only one person who could fulfill its requirements. God was working a plan that was in place from before the foundation of the world. The calling of the

nation Israel and the establishment of its laws and
rites of worship were set in place not because God
hadn't thought of anything better. Rather, He was
allowing the drama of human history to unfold to
establish unequivocally that nothing could be done
through human effort to bridge the gap sin had created. There could only be one way. One man.

The writer of Hebrews says it best,

> Therefore, when Christ came into the world,
> . . . first he said: "Sacrifices and offerings,
> burnt offerings and sin offerings you did
> not desire, nor were you pleased with them"
> (although the law required them to be
> made). Then he said, "Here I am, I have come
> to do your will." He sets aside the first to
> establish the second. And by that will, we
> have been made holy through the sacrifice
> of the body of Jesus Christ once for all. Day
> after day every priest stands and performs
> his religious duties; again and again he
> offers the same sacrifices, which can never
> take away sins. But when this priest had
> offered for all time one sacrifice for sins, he
> sat down at the right hand of God. Since

that time he waits for his enemies to be made his footstool, because by one sacrifice he has made perfect forever those who are being made holy (Heb. 10:5,8-14).

Worship in the Shadow of the Cross

Worship is not a result of our moving toward God, it is our response to His overture of grace toward us. To remove confidence in the finished atoning work of Christ on our behalf is to shift the focus from Christ to us, thus marring the beauty of worship. There can be no room for Gnosticism and elitism: All must come to the place where the mountains have been leveled and the valleys have been raised up to a level footing in the shadow of the Cross. Here is where God walks. Here is where He dwells.

The Cross stands front and center in Zion. Without the Cross, there is no true worship. To see God is to see Him here, on the Cross. This reality is at the center of our devotion. This is our King, and we ignore this Man of Sorrows at our own peril.

And now, to all eternity, the cross remains at the heart of God, stands as the truest symbol of God, offers the most exact and precise exposition of God. Part of the point of the doctrine of the Trinity is that what happened to Jesus of Nazareth . . . happened to God; and, having happened to God, it has, so to speak, made God decisively and in practice, once and for all, what he always was in principle. That is why, on Good Friday, those who come to church do so, not to venerate a piece of wood . . . but to use the cross as the truest possible icon of the living and loving God. As with any icon, the point is to look through it at the reality, of which like all true symbols, the cross speaks more deeply than words.[3]

New Testament Sacrifice of Praise

We must see Zion with New Testament faith, understanding that the once and for all work of Christ is our confidence, and nothing else. The only remaining sacrifice now is the "sacrifice of praise" (Heb. 13:15). This is not about forcing an outward expression of worship when we just don't feel like singing; it is about the continuous fruit of our lives. We have abandoned all to follow this King and have confessed Jesus as Lord. Now He has become everything to us as our source of salvation. Our whole lives have now become expressions of worship that go far beyond words, and all of life has become a living sacrifice (see Rom. 12:1). This is the only reasonable worship.

The Lord's Supper

Observance of the Lord's Supper is a key to keeping this in focus. For some, its observance is sporadic, and usually tacked on to the end of a service. For others, who partake on a more consistent basis, it can become passé, and even boring. Our worship suffers greatly unless we cultivate a focused and passionate remembrance of Christ's death. If we fail in this, we may be in danger of emptying the Cross of its power (see 1 Cor. 1:17-18). Paul seemed to be very concerned that an abuse of its adherence was causing sickness and even death in the community (see 1 Cor. 11:27-30).

There is something powerful in the breaking of the bread and the drinking of the symbol of His blood that pushes us beyond the confines of liturgy. To hold the symbols in our hands, and to taste and imbibe, invokes something powerful. We must rediscover the mystery, power and simplicity of this ancient sacrament, for it lies at the very core of our worship expression and is the basis upon which we gather.

> Therefore, [friends], since we have confidence to enter the Most Holy Place by the blood of Jesus, by a new and living way opened for us through the curtain, that is, his body, and since we have a great priest over the house of God, let us draw near to God. . . . Let us not give up meeting together, as some are in the habit of doing, but let us encourage one another—and all the more as you see the Day approaching (Heb. 10:19-22,25).

WORSHIP AS COMMUNITY

The Lord loves the gates of Zion
PSALM 87:1

There is power in gathering to worship, for it is here that God delights to dwell. He has sacrificed His all to make it so. He loves the gates of Zion more than any other place.

For those who live in Western cultures that emphasize the individual, it is hard to grasp the centrality of gathering to scriptural worship. The worship God seeks has gathering at its heart. The journey into worship is a journey into community. Beyond obligation or guilt, there is a Spirit-birthed longing to join our lives and voices together in worship before God. There are things to be discovered in the corporate place of worship that can never be unlocked in our personal prayer closet or personal worship space, as powerful as those times are.

In our struggle to fight against empty liturgy and what can become the vain repetition of church life, we must not lose the power of gathering. When we worship together, what we experience is not just a concert vibe or crowd dynamics. God dwells with worshipping people.

For many on the Earth, the coming together for worship is at risk of their lives. In spite of living in an environment hostile toward Christianity, thousands of Christ's followers gather to worship God.

I'll never forget my first experience in a Third World culture. I ended up at a gathering in north East India with underground church leaders from all across the Himalayan Mountains. Many had walked for days and suffered incredible hardship on the way.

Some would return home to houses burned to the ground by angry priests or political rebels taking advantage of their absence.

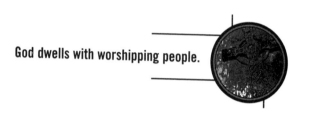

God dwells with worshipping people.

Though there was desire for teaching and encouragement, the thing they longed for most was worship. The more we worshipped, the more they wanted to understand. As we moved beyond liturgies and songs that had come from Western influence, the songs and expression of their hearts bled through, and the presence of God increased in such a mighty way that we were all in awe. Again and again the cry for worship filled us as the delight in God's heart to meet with us overwhelmed our agendas and plans for the day.

Is this just empty fanaticism, or religious zeal?

At this hour the mystical teaching of these words is plain. God delights in the prayers and praises of Christian families and individuals, but he has a special eye to the assemblies of the faithful, and he has a special delight in their devotions in their church capacity. The great festivals, when the crowds surrounded the temple gates, were fair in the Lord's eyes, and even such is the general assembly and church of the first-born whose names are written in heaven.[4]

This one was born in Zion
PSALM 87:4

Worship is a God-initiated invitation to the gates of Zion. This is a place of great privilege—an encounter that even the angelic host of heaven cannot comprehend and must only watch with wonder. This is a place for those who are born here.

I tell you the truth, no one can enter the kingdom of God unless he is born of water and the Spirit. You should not be surprised at my saying, "You must be born again" (John 3:5,7).

Living by Grace

Something changes in the very core of a human being when touched by grace. The heavy yoke of legalism is shattered. The propensity to atone for our brokenness through religious activity wanes, swallowed up in mercy. Idolatry loses its grip under the power of this kind of freedom. Worship is no longer just an activity—it is now our identity. As Jesus would tell us, God longs for worshippers (not just worship) and those born into worship are those He seeks (see John 4:23).

It's like learning to walk, breathe, eat—to live—for the very first time. It is a fresh start and there is nothing we add to this new experience of worship. Christ has done it all; we can bring nothing to add to His work. Surrendering under His majesty and grace in this place of Kingdom worship is all that is left. We are born again.

One's DNA is now branded by worship, and this inner work produces a worshipper. Impassioned by mercy, something is released in us that religious experience alone cannot touch. No longer are we trying to attain to something in God's presence—we have become worshippers by His grace. It has become our very nature to worship. This will be our character long past the end of time as we know it. We will worship forever. We have been born in Zion.

To know God and to be written in His book is equated in the Psalms with being "born in Zion."[5]

I will record Rahab and Babylon among those
who acknowledge me–Philistia too, and Tyre,
along with Cush . . . The Lord will write in the reg-
ister of the peoples: "This one was born in Zion."

PSALM 87:4,6

Walking in Freedom

This liberation knows no bounds. Under God's kingdom reign, people will be drawn from every tongue,
tribe and nation. Pagan and Jewish alike will come,
no longer bearing the citizenship of any earthly
nation but as citizens of Zion. Race, economic status,
lineage, gender, age, language, education hold no
qualification in this place. Only one thing gets you
in, and it is open to all who would receive it. To clear
immigration, you must hold heaven's papers pur-
chased by the blood of Christ and bearing the seal of
the Holy Spirit. One by one the passports of Zion are
matched up to the eternal book of register, the
Lamb's book of life.

If you could catch a glimpse of the names written
in this Lamb's book (see Rev. 21:27),[6] beside each one
you would see: "this one was born in Zion"; "this one
was born in Zion"; "this one was born in Zion." To be
a born-again people is to stand shoulder to shoulder,

heart to heart with redeemed people from every nation under heaven exercising our one common birthright—worship.

Our birth certificates and passports now come from a city of unearthly origin. Along the path of life this side of heaven, the Kingdom invades our present reality, and worship is sweet. But we are not foolish enough to stop here and put our roots down on the earth. Just as the people of Israel longed, and some still are waiting for the establishment of the Temple in Jerusalem, so our hearts long for the place of eternal worship, the heavenly Jerusalem, the city of God. The place where all is revealed, darkness is banished, and every tear is wiped from our eyes (see Rev. 7:17).

> *As they make music they will sing,*
> *"All my fountains are in you."*
>
> PSALM 87:7

"ALL MY FOUNTAINS ARE IN YOU"

So our music is filled with the theme "All my fountains are in you" (Ps. 87:7). Worship is life to us. Just as an artesian spring bubbles up from the earth and becomes a source of life to everything it touches, so worship is our spring, our fountain. To stay away from here will bring dehydration, dryness and eventually death. For the one born in Zion, the place of worship is the place of life.

The fountains in Psalm 87:7, however, speak not only of the place of worship but also of the focus of our worship. Jesus, the Light of the world and the One who rules in this kingdom of Light, is our source of life, our fountain.

As we gather, we foreshadow the reality of eternal worship. We come to the King on His throne under the banner of love. We worship not just as something we do but because of who we are by the work of Christ.

The psalmist is clear. We will make music. But what will characterize the songs of the redeemed are songs birthed in the spirit of worship—songs that acknowledge Zion and the King who dwells there as the source of inspiration and life. As we make music, we will sing, "All my fountains are in you, O God."

There is a worship that God seeks, and it is found here—in Zion.

Chapter Three

BY THE SPIRIT

The gift of "charismatic worship" to the church has been functionally to restore the Holy Spirit to our services. Charismatic worship, then finds its source in the Father, is mediated through the Son, and is empowered and led by the Spirit. . . . True charismatic worship is not human-centered or emotion-centered. The Spirit comes to bear witness to Christ (John 15:26) and empowers and directs the church to that end. Honoring the Son honors the Father and keeps charismatic worship from becoming Unitarian or Binitarian by neglecting one member of the Trinity for another.

—DON WILLIAMS, *EXPLORING THE WORSHIP SPECTRUM*

Just as the journey into Zion is a supernatural work, the whole worship experience is sustained by the Holy Spirit. To worship without the presence and empowering of the Spirit is not New Testament worship. The worship God seeks is Spirit led.

Music, art and liturgy carry a power that can touch the human soul and create a sense of awe; yet void of the Spirit, this alone worship is not true worship in the biblical sense. It may be steeped in tradition and anchored in flawless theology, but without the Spirit's breath it is vain repetition. It may reflect the culture of the times and give an accessible expression of song and art for the gathered church and the world that is watching, but without the Spirit of God weaving through the melodies, it is not a sound that reaches the ear of God, nor a place where He can dwell. Flesh gives birth to flesh, but the Spirit gives birth to spirit.

Without the influence of God's Spirit, man has to rely on his own subjectivity to provide the creative force. Often he tries to achieve this by transgressing all intellectual and moral boundaries, giving free reign to his passions, perhaps using drinking or drugs to stimulate his subjectivity.[1]

The worshipper's journey is one steeped in faith and is not sustained through hype and external stimulant. It is a faith that embraces that which we cannot see, making the work of the Spirit indispensable. Our tendency is to center our worship on symbol and liturgy, but this is not the beginning place for true Christian worship.

The inherent human capacity for concept and symbol formation is recognized as a fundamental and necessary element in the human understanding, anticipation, and creation of reality. The mind is not the passive reflector of an external world and its intrinsic order, but is active and creative in the process of perception and cognition. Reality is in some sense constructed by the mind, not simply perceived by it, and many such constructions are possible, none necessarily sovereign.[2]

Yet there is a reality we reach for that cannot be comprehended by the human mind. There is a reality outside of our own perception and cognition. We can only see this reality with the eyes of spiritual understanding.

Paul refers to this tension when he writes to the church in Corinth. He wrestles with the mystical and the practical in both prayer and worship:

> What shall I do? I will pray with my spirit, but I will also pray with my mind; I will sing with my spirit, but I will also sing with my mind. If you are praising God with your spirit, how can one who finds himself among those who do not understand say "Amen" to your thanksgiving, since he does not know what you are saying? (1 Cor. 14:15-16).

Worship does create tension. But to deal with it by eradicating the place of the Spirit in worship is to turn it into something less than God intended. In fact, it removes Him from the experience, for the Holy Spirit is God. Whatever the liturgy, whatever the expression of song, whatever the preaching or ministry that is engaged in, a key to the worship that God desires is the work of the Spirit.

THE HOLY SPIRIT IN WORSHIP

There are several indicators in the New Testament that point us to the central role of the Holy Spirit in the worship of the Church.

Worship Is a Mark of the True Church

Paul makes a striking observation about the Church. It is marked by worship. Just as surely as circumcision marked the male gender of Israel as a sign of covenant, so the mark of the Church, the true circumcision, is that of worship.

The Church had been birthed into something that was beyond the experience of Judaism, and certainly was unlike any of the pagan religions and philosophies of the day. In Philippians 3:3, Paul makes the observation that the worship of this peculiar people emerging on the earth was unique. It is by the Spirit of God.

The reference here is fascinating, as Paul does not use a common New Testament word for "worship" in this passage. He moves from the more personal *proskenueo* to the more liturgical and corporate word *latrueo*, denoting that believers must worship together, but the nature of their liturgy is that it is Spirit led.

The worship of the Church is a work of the Spirit that results in glory being given to Jesus, and an activity that places no confidence in the flesh. It is a supernatural activity focused on Christ.

This does not demand the immediate conclusion that all such worship is spontaneous and unplanned (although there is room for that), but rather that in all facets of planning and execution, the direction of the Holy Spirit is sought.

Also, it creates the sense that the worship experience is one in which the expectation of encounter is critical. This is not empty ritual, but an event in which we encounter the living God. The Holy Spirit is not a force to be coerced and manipulated in order to heighten our human senses and make worship more delightful. He is a vibrant and real Person of the Trinity whose delight it is to bring connection with the Father and a revelation of the Son. He is intrinsically involved in the process of worship, bringing revelation, inspiring song and empowering community.

Worship Music Is Born from the Spirit's Infilling

The music of the New Testament church, the most central expression of which is the vocalized song, was to be cultivated from a posture of the Spirit's infilling. Again, we turn to the teachings of Paul, this time his letter to the Ephesians.

Do not get drunk on wine, which leads to debauchery. Instead, be filled with the Spirit. Speak to one another with psalms, hymns and spiritual songs. Sing and make music in [*from*] your heart to the Lord, always giving thanks to God the Father for everything, in the name of our Lord Jesus Christ (Eph. 5:18-20).

The inference of the passage is that the songs are related to the injunction to be filled with the Spirit. An encounter with the Holy Spirit results in song. (The parallel passage in Colossians 3:16 indicates that a sense of being filled with the word of Christ has the same result.)

Expressed worship through song is a work of the Spirit. This is not only about musical skill or tastes. If one is filled, the text is clear, one will sing. To ignore this aspect of life in the Spirit and community will hamper the expression of communal worship and stunt the spiritual growth of the individual.

The Ephesians passage makes us aware of a key aspect of worship in community. We speak to *each other* with psalms, hymns and spiritual songs. There is a strengthening that comes to the Church through the release of song. Part of the strength that we receive in coming together is through worship that is empowered by the Spirit.

Spirit-Filled Worship Leads Us to the Father

It is clear from the life of Christ that a key aspect of His ministry is to lead us to the Father. Jesus' relationship with His Father was central in His life. Christ's whole identity and ministry flowed from this place of intimacy, the ability to cry "Abba, Father." This kind of nearness to God was something very unique; and as modeled by Jesus, it had a tremendous impact on the expression of worship in the emerging Church. Christ would make it very clear in John 4:21-24 that true worshippers, the ones whom God seeks, worship the Father.

Paul, once again, illuminates our understanding regarding the work of the Spirit in our being able to cultivate this kind of relationship with God, which is at the core of our worship. He states in Romans,

> [You] who are led by the Spirit of God are sons [and daughters] of God. For you did not receive a spirit that makes you a slave again to fear, but you received the Spirit of sonship.

And by him we cry, "Abba, Father." The Spirit himself testifies with our spirit that we are God's children (Rom. 8:14-16).

I have rarely seen anything quench worship more than the dark side of fear that paralyzes people in their relationship with God. When trust is damaged, and the "Abba" cry is shut down, worship dries up. It is only a work of the Spirit that can reignite this connection with God. As Paul emphasizes: By the Spirit, we cry "Abba, Father."

I remember being in a worship gathering in the nation of Thailand. It was my responsibility to give the teaching at one of the sessions, and I was teaching from the above passage. Every time I said "Abba," or "Father," however, I would get this twinge in my gut and a sense that something was wrong. It took me the longest time to figure it out. Finally I stopped the teaching and turned to the translator to inquire how he was translating these words. He told me the Thai word for "God" that he was using and gave me an explanation of it. It had nothing at all to do with the concept of a father. I gently challenged him, and he informed me that there was no word they could use in their culture that was appropriate for God as

I had described Him. You couldn't just call Him "Father." That was against their culture and their understanding of Christianity. I asked him what word was used when we sang hymns or songs that used the word "Father" to refer to God. It was the same word. And, again, it did not convey the heart of the Scriptures at all.

I was baffled and unsure as to what to do. I simply stated that I was neither a linguist nor a missiologist, but that to ignore this as one of the ways to address and approach God was unbiblical. I explained that during the writing of the New Testament, new words had to be formed to describe aspects of the faith. New language had to be found to express new truth. Maybe this was true for the Thai people as well. I implored them to ask the Holy Spirit how to call out "Abba, Father."

I no sooner had said this than a woman somewhere in the gathering cried out something that sounded to me like "Papa." It was from such a deep place that it almost sounded like a shriek. Something broke. People began to weep and moan. Tears were abundant, and many fell to the ground. I am certain that demonic deliverance was happening as the cry of the Spirit testifying with the cry of their spirits rang out across the auditorium. I have rarely seen anything like it. Needless to say, our worship went to a whole new depth, and many were set free that day.

The Spirit's Revelation in Worship

Another work of the Spirit that is critical in the worship journey is that of revelation.

> The Spirit searches all things, even the deep things of God. For who among [people] knows the thoughts of a [person] except the [person's] spirit within him [or her]? In the same way no one knows the thoughts of God except the Spirit of God. We have not received the spirit of the world but the Spirit who is from God, that we may understand what God has freely given us (1 Cor. 2:10-12).

God is at the center of our worship. Without the work of the Holy Spirit, we cannot understand who He is and what He has so freely given us. This truth must be more than just mental assent. We must intentionally request of the Holy Spirit His work in our understanding and in our offering of worship to God. His work—and His work alone—transforms our liturgy into praise, our songs into worship, and our lives of mundane dualism into living sacrifices that see God glorified in all that we say and do.

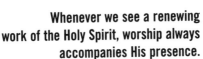

Whenever we see a renewing work of the Holy Spirit, worship always accompanies His presence.

Whenever we see a renewing work of the Holy Spirit, worship always accompanies His presence. He does bring empowered preaching and an impact that shakes society to its very core, but resonating at the heart of it all is a new song. John Wesley had Charles. Dwight Moody had Sankey. Billy Sunday had Rodeheaver. Billy Graham has Cliff Barrows. There were the songs of the Welsh revival, the Finney revival, and on and on it goes. Where the Spirit of God has free reign, the worship of the saints will emerge. You can't stop the song.

DEPENDENT ON THE SPIRIT

We must learn dependence on the Holy Spirit. Whatever our struggles with a more "charismatic" approach to church liturgy, recognition of the place of the Spirit in all functions of gathered community and His role in our living a life of worship is paramount.

We find that as the Spirit of the Lord has liberty, all aspects of community gathering are impacted. Worship is kept fresh and relevant, not based on the style of presentation or liturgical style, but by the presence of the Spirit. The injection of fresh life into our worship gatherings is not just an overhaul of production or the use of a guitar as opposed to an organ. The place to begin is a cry for the Spirit.

It must be said, however, that the Spirit is more than just a facilitator of worship. He is fully a member of the Trinity and must be revered as such. He is God: "The Christian doctrine of the Trinity boldly declares the equality of the Three Persons and the right of the Holy Spirit to be worshipped and glorified. Anything less than this is something less than Trinitarian."[3] We honor His presence and role in worship as much as that of the Father and the Son.

This insight is one that the Church constantly needs to cultivate. The prayer of Paul for the Church, in Ephesians 1:17, is an unrelenting request to "the glorious Father" for "the Spirit of wisdom and revelation." The desire of this apostle for wisdom and insight is not self-promoting and based on a longing for the Church to be more impressive in its liturgy and spiritual experiences. The whole goal of Paul's prayer is that the Church might move into a deeper knowledge of God, beyond theology, into a wisdom anchored in the deep knowing of relationship. This goal cannot be attained apart from the work of Spirit, for wisdom and revelation are "possible only as the gift of the Spirit who makes wise, and who alone reveals the truth."[4]

We cannot discover the worship God is seeking apart from the working of the Holy Spirit in our lives. We must submit to His guidance and leadership in all aspects of worship, both as gathered community and in our individual paths of life. Just as we do not know how to pray (see Rom. 8:26), so we must rely on the work of the Spirit in us to draw from us the worship in which God delights.

Chapter Four

SPIRIT AND TRUTH

A time is coming and has now come.

JOHN 4:23

In exploring the worship that is led by the Spirit, one thing becomes clear. Spirit gives birth to spirit, and flesh to flesh. As we encounter more of God together, a worship that is not contained by rote liturgy or housed in buildings of human construct begins to emerge. The status quo is in serious jeopardy. Solomon, the wisest one to ever live, realized this, even as he dedicated the Temple: "But will God really dwell on the earth? The heavens, even the highest heaven, cannot contain you. How much less this temple I have built!" (1 Kings 8:27).

God's search for worship is an intense one. Jesus refers to it in John 4:19-23 in His dialogue with a woman longing to understand the worship that is beyond mountains and temples and which could satisfy her deepest thirst. The Greek is *zeteo* which means "to seek or strive after, endeavor, to desire."[1] This seeking is not the pining of a jilted lover or the selfish tantrum of one who cannot have what he or she wants. It is a passionate fire that is self-initiated and sustained from a place of holy zeal beyond human comprehension. As a result, to go to the place that God is seeking in worship can take us beyond what is comfortable.

Yet a time is coming and has now come when the true worshipers will worship the Father in spirit and truth, for they are the kind of worshipers the Father seeks. God is spirit, and his worshipers must worship in spirit and in truth (John 4:23-24).

The dynamics of true worship take place in an element beyond anything that we know as natural. God is Spirit.

He is a spirit and no physical representation can capture him. This separates him from the dumb idols who neither speak nor act, and, as he says to Moses, because of his glory, no one can see his face and live (Exod. 33:20). Unlike earthly kings who filled their temples with statues of the gods, then, the Lord keeps the holy of holies in his temple empty, except for the Ark of the Covenant with its vacant mercy seat, and the She-kinah, the glory of his presence which comes and goes (see 1 Kings 8:10-11 and Ezekiel 10:18,19). This confirms that God is an invisible spirit who is transcendent and rules over all.[2]

UNDERSTANDING TRUE WORSHIP

To come into His presence is not a meeting of the minds or a matching of wills. This is not just one physical presence dominating another. No, the arena of this worship is in the place of spirit where God encounters humanity in the rawness of His presence and the vulnerability of our brokenness. God is spirit, and to worship Him is to touch something that is, without a doubt, spiritual.

Those who are identified as "true worshipers" will not offer their worship in the same way they offer praise in any other arena. This is something that transcends the adulation reserved for rock stars, athletes and the other icons of our age. This is far beyond any loyalty that any earthly king or leader could ever command.

Drinking Deeply of the Living Water

Here we come full circle again to the work of the Cross and the need for the indwelling Holy Spirit. Outside of Christ, the part of our being that true worship springs from is a place that is as dry and dead as the crusted surface of a dry lake bed or empty well. No life at all. We must have the atoning blood of Christ washing us and His living water springing up inside of us unto eternal life—for without them we are lifeless in trespasses and sin.

At times we may try to create the illusion that we are alive through the psychedelic fantasies that are awakened through drugs or through the numbing of alcohol that gives us false courage to step out of ourselves. The ecstasy of sexual encounters and pornographic voyeurism may create a sense of life for a time as well. But the dark truth remains: We are dead in sin, longing to be alive. Though we may convince ourselves that we are drinking deep of living water, all that is left in our mouths is sand. It is a thirst that will never be quenched apart from the living water of Christ.

Persevering in Worship

Once redeemed, to stay in true worship can be challenging as well. Through the ebb and flow of life and the distractions upon the modern Church, our worship can begin to slide away from its true source and become empty. Our praise can become hype and our worship simply an identifying with feelings of nostalgia and "God bumps." In an attempt to convince ourselves that we are "in" the Spirit or "anointed"—we can create illusions of spirituality. We may even begin to drink again of things that sustained false worship before we came to know God. The result is something counterfeit.

Connecting with Our Father

The end of worship is to connect with God, not to get in touch with ourselves. And yet if we truly become the worshippers that God seeks, we will become more alive and real in the experience than we ever could be anywhere else.

John 4:23 demands reflection here. God is called Father, *pater* in the Greek. When this word is used of God in the New Testament, it is used in relation to those who have been born anew (see John 1:12-13).[3] The human subjects of this Ruler and those who populate His kingdom are not just vassals or slaves. The King has become Father; and through rebirth and adoption, grace and regeneration (for only Christ is the begotten of God), those who bear this work of the Spirit upon them are His children.

It is here that we can be vulnerable and real under the safety of this Father's love. To give Him what He seeks is to become who we are destined to be.

I long to dwell in your tent forever and take refuge in the shelter of your wings (Ps. 61:4).

He who dwells in the shelter of the Most High will rest in the shadow of the Almighty. I will say of the LORD, "He is my refuge and my fortress, my God, in whom I trust." Surely he will save you from the fowler's snare and from the deadly pestilence. He will cover you with his feathers, and under his wings you will find refuge; his faithfulness will be your shield and rampart (Ps. 91:1-4).

Then the LORD will create over all of Mount Zion and over those who assemble there a cloud of smoke by day and a glow of flaming fire by night; over all the glory will be a canopy. It will be a shelter and shade from the heat of the day, and a refuge and hiding place from the storm and rain (Isa. 4:5-6).

And so the mystery of the worship God seeks goes deeper. We come in full of recognition of His majesty and power, and yet as sons and daughters. Our definitions of worship now must embrace a new dimension of understanding. The King has become Father.

Under this sovereign gaze we are called to be more vulnerable than we have ever been before. We must step past all the wounding and pain that the broken fathers of the earth have inflicted on us and learn to trust again. The call to worship is a call to come home—and to hide nothing from our God. He challenges us to move beyond outward compliance and the protocol of proper behavior in the courts of the King. He wants something deeper.

Recognizing That We Worship in Spirit and in Truth

What is the worship that this Father seeks from those who are truly His children? What is worship for those who have been born in Zion and now gather in that place filled and empowered by the Spirit of God?

> True worship will reflect our deepest perceptions, reflections, feelings and desires. God is so secure within Himself, and His covenant love is so unbreakable, that we can be secure in self-disclosure.

Those who worship Him must worship in spirit and truth. This is far from some rare mystical experience only to be attained by monks and priests. It is a worship that is full of the grit and reality of life as we hide nothing from the Father and trust fully in Him.

The spirit is the *pneuma*,[4] that immaterial, invisible part of us, the sentient element within all of us by which we perceive, reflect, feel and desire. It is perhaps here that we most reflect the image of God branded on all people, for God is spirit. True worship will reflect our deepest perceptions, reflections, feelings and desires. God is so secure within Himself, and His covenant love is so unbreakable, that we can be secure in self-disclosure. This is unlike any other relationship that we can engage in. We are not embroiled in a dysfunctional codependency. Rather, we are surrendered in complete trust: The One who has no need desires our lives. The One who is holy invites us to come as we are and cast ourselves upon His mercy.

The true worshippers worship from this kind of vulnerability. This cannot be compared to a self-help posture of actualization, but it is an awareness of the truth that the more we expose ourselves before God, trusting in the love of our Father, the more we are changed in the encounter. Our perceptions begin to line up with His sovereign vantage point over history and the path that our lives take. Our reflections become more and more musings of Him than of our own opinions and attitudes. Our feelings do not diminish, nor do we submerge them under a religious cloak; but they are released under His watchful eye and are tamed by His love for us. Our desires become His desires. The dynamism of Romans 12:1-2 no longer is something out of reach; rather, from the place of this kind of worship, it is as real to us as the air we breathe:

> Therefore, I urge you, brothers [and sisters], in view of God's mercy, to offer your bodies as living sacrifices, holy and pleasing to God—this is your spiritual act of worship. Do not conform any longer to the pattern of this world, but be transformed by the renewing of your mind. Then you will be able to test and approve what God's will is—his good, pleasing and perfect will.

Truth as described in John 4 is *alethia*, a truth that is not merely verbal but one of sincerity and integrity of character, the reality lying at the basis of an appearance; the manifested, veritable essence of a matter.[5] Here nothing is counterfeit. Nothing is hidden or glossed over. Again, we have the striking pose of complete honesty and a picture of worship that is uncomfortable in its vulnerability.

We Worship in Joy and in Sorrow

With this understanding of worship, there is room for the lament as well as for the songs of joy. The exposing of doubts and fears is not a demonstration of a lack of faith, but rather an honest wrestling before the King. There will be those who grieve in Zion, and in this place of humble worship they will find "a crown of beauty instead of ashes, the oil of gladness instead of mourning, and a garment of praise instead of a spirit of despair" (Isa. 61:3).

As I am writing these words, I am keenly aware of the struggle in my own soul. To be this raw and real before God seems to violate my sense of propriety regarding the posture that I am to take before almighty God. I continue to discover that "far from competing with each other, intimacy and reverence actually go hand in hand."[6]

My thoughts go back to times when I have watched close friends and people that I've worked with die. Not the dignified deaths of those who have lived full and meaningful lives, but untimely deaths caused by cancer and other diseases. I am sad as I reflect upon the demise of my friends who never made it free of the inner-city streets, as death caught up to them through murder, abuse and suicide.

I correspond and visit with many friends in the places of the earth where religious freedom is a dream, and many suffer and are martyred for their journey in Jesus.

How do we worship here? We come not with the platitudes of the latest contemporary chorus, hanging on to distant truth that rests only in the mind. Only spirit and truth will suffice, and we are amazed by the Father's willingness to let the sounds of sorrow bleed through the melodies of praise.

The heretical tendency to live life as two people, sacred and secular, the "real me" and the "holy me," sucks the life out of worship. This mind-set allows the leaven of the Pharisees to permeate life and liturgy, and this worship illusion is something that God cannot receive. It is the invitation to come in spirit and truth that sets us free from this Christian schizophrenia, liberating us to be real.

FOLLOWING THE EXAMPLE OF JESUS

No one exemplifies true worship better than Jesus. Being fully God, He was fully man, and from His place of humanity He faced what any human would ever face. He unlocked the mystery of spirit and truth like no other.

He knew the inexpressible joy of the Father over His life and lived in that reality, yet He faced the suffering of those around Him, and that of His own path, with a sobriety and depth that is quite breathtaking. His prayer life was marked by loud wailings and tears, and His path into obedience was sign posted with suffering the whole way. We see Him in the Garden of Gethsemane sweating great drops of blood; so honest were His confessions of agony before His God that He begged for the cup of sorrow to be taken from Him. This was no lack of faith nor a brother in need of a little joy. With surrender free of empty religious jargon and vain repetition, He bent His will to that of the Father and gave all for the glory of God and the freedom of humankind (see Matt. 26:39). This was spirit and truth lived out in a most vulnerable and accessible way, a model for all who would follow Him to the Father.

We must allow ourselves to understand more and more the One whom we worship and His desires. If we do not fully trust Him and allow Him to define worship for us, we will never get to this place of spirit and truth.

God is not threatened by our sin and brokenness. His love is not so fragile that it will break under the strain of our darkest secrets and betrayals. To hide them is folly, for He knows all anyway. To attempt worship that is free of pain and struggle is impossible and would make a mockery of the Cross. We must simply come. Just as we are, fully recognizing the King before whom we bow, we walk into the depths of relationship that He calls us to as our Father.

God not only invites such disarming intimacy, He seeks it. Those who worship Him must worship in spirit and truth.

Chapter Five

CREATION, CREATIVITY AND THE NATIONS

Art is not a religion, not an activity relegated to a chosen few, nor a mere worldly, superfluous affair. None of these views of art does justice to the creativity with which God has endowed man. It is the ability to make something beautiful (as well as useful), just as God made the world beautiful and said, "It is good." Art as such needs no justification; rather, it demands a response, like that of the twenty-four elders in Revelation who worship God just one . . . for . . . the very act of creation itself:

> *You are worthy, our Lord and God, To receive glory and honor and power, For you created all things, And by your will they were created And have their being. (Revelation 4:11)*

—H. R. ROOKMAAKER, *THE CREATIVE GIFT, ESSAYS ON ART AND THE CHRISTIAN LIFE*

God is Creator—an artist of such passionate genius that He creates out of nothing, ex nihilo, and does so as a free act. He is the only being in the universe who is truly original, and He creates for His good pleasure.[1] God does not create under the commissioning of another; He does not create out of need; nor is He compelled by an insecure desire to impress. He creates because it is in His nature, and it is His delight to do so.

> "Where were you when I laid the foundation of the earth? Tell me, if you have understanding. Who determined its measurements—surely you know! Who stretched the line upon it? On what were its bases sunk, or who laid its cornerstone, *when the morning stars sang together and all the sons of God (angels) shouted for joy?*"

Do you see the picture? No man was there. So Job should humble himself and realize there are a few things he (and we!) may not understand. But in making this point God cannot resist, it seems, mentioning what the mood of heaven was like at the moment of creation. "All the sons of God shouted for joy." All the angels had evidently been created before the universe. And it is not hard to see why. God meant there to be an audience when he created the world. I am sure he said, "Watch this!" when he spoke the galaxies into existence. Imagine the awe and wonder that exploded among the angels. They had never seen or even imagined matter. They are all "ministering *spirits*" (Hebrews 1:14) and have no material bodies as we do. When God brought utterly unheard of qualities of sight and sound and smell and touch and taste, this was totally unknown to the angels. God had made it all up. It was not like the unveiling of a new painting made of all the colors and paints we are all familiar with. It was absolutely, totally, unimaginably new! And the response of the sons of God was to shout for joy.[2]

CREATION IS A GLIMPSE OF GOD

As with any true artist, God has poured so much of Himself into creation that if we look carefully enough at the work of His hands, we can see Him. This is not to say that God is "in" creation as would be the worldview of a New Ager or animist but rather to say that His mark is indelibly upon His creation. In fact, creation alone is evidence enough of God's existence. As a result, there is not one person anywhere and from any time period that has not had a chance to embrace the true God in faith.

> The wrath of God is being revealed from heaven against all the godlessness and wickedness of [persons] who suppress the truth by their wickedness, since what may be known about God is plain to them, because God has made it plain to them. For since the creation of the world God's invisible qualities—his eternal power and divine nature— have been clearly seen, being understood from what has been made, so that [people] are without excuse (Rom. 1:18-20).

It would seem from the text above that, for the seeking heart, the evidence of God is in plain sight. Creation is not designed to be a Rubik's Cube or a cosmic riddle that only the spiritually elite can solve. God has made it plain. The natural things speak of the invisible. Cultures that have roots in appreciation and awareness of nature will have embedded in their psyches an innate understanding of a Creator and all-supreme Being. Creation is God's ultimate apologetic.

CREATION EXISTS TO DELIGHT GOD

It is a marvelous thing that God, who is spirit, would delight in the creation of a natural realm. The unseen God creates too many stars for the eyes to see and a range of colors and motion that weave through plants, animals, birds and reptiles that is astounding. God has looked over all that He has made and has declared it as good—even "very good"

Creation exists not merely for humanity, for our enjoyment and purposes; its highest purpose is for the delight of God.

as He gazed at the man and woman He had created in His own image (see Gen. 1:24,27-31). He rejoices in His works (see Ps. 104). Creation exists not merely for humanity, for our enjoyment and purposes;

its highest purpose is for the delight of God.

I have often reflected upon the vastness of creation. Scientists are constantly discovering new species of life. Each time we develop lenses that can cast our gaze deeper into space, we discover more stars and swirling galaxies than we ever dreamed were possible. We have yet to plumb the ocean depths, and we know that there are creatures moving about in that watery darkness that no human eye has ever seen. The depth and mystery of it all is overwhelming. What's it all there for? It has been created for the enjoyment of God.

CREATION PLAYS A CRUCIAL ROLE IN WORSHIP

Inspiring a Deeper Worship of the Creator

Just as creation is there for God, so then my exploration of it should lead me to a deeper place of worship. Often, worship songwriters will ask me how to pull out of a slump or how to move beyond clichés in their writing. Several times I have challenged them to pull out an *Encyclopedia Britannica* or watch a few National Geographic specials to see what inspiration comes from creation.

Solomon discovered this source of creativity.

God gave Solomon wisdom and very great insight, and a breadth of understanding as measureless as the sand on the seashore. Solomon's wisdom was greater than the wisdom of all the men of the East, and greater than all the wisdom of Egypt. He was wiser than any other man, including Ethan the Ezrahite—wiser than Heman, Calcol and Darda, the sons of Mahol. And his fame spread to all the surrounding nations. He spoke three thousand proverbs and his songs numbered a thousand and five. He described plant life, from the cedar of Lebanon to the hyssop that grows out of walls. He also taught about animals and birds, reptiles and fish. Men of all nations came to listen to Solomon's wisdom, sent by all the kings of the world, who had heard of his wisdom (1 Kings 4:29-34).

Lending Beauty and Diversity to Our Worship

It is critical to note here that God does not pit the natural realm against that of the spirit. In fact, one reflects the other. The worship God seeks is not divorced from the senses, as He created the realm in which these things thrive. Creation itself expresses praise to God (see Ps. 148), so it would make sense that we who are created in His image should express worship that captures the passion and the diverse expressions of creativity. To fill our liturgy with creativity and artistry is not earthly but rather an appropriate offering of praise.

REVELATION PROVIDES A GLIMPSE OF THRONE ROOM WORSHIP

It is no wonder, then, that the worship around God's throne is vibrant. The worship expressed right in the very presence of God's throne is a visual and sonic display of pageantry that cannot be duplicated on Earth. Revelation 4 gives us a peek into this worship experience in the throne room.

God, the King upon His throne, has colors rippling through His being. As we see God on His throne, He is not just simply some white blazing light; but as John the Revelator struggles to describe the God he has seen, he tells us "the one who sat there had the appearance of jasper and carnelian" (Rev. 4:3). God is colorful. Jasper is a transparent stone, offering to the eye a variety of the most vivid colors; and the carnelian, or sardine-stone, is red. There is symbolism to the colors of these stones, but just the fact that there is a visual impact of color upon seeing God is amazing. The reality that the being of God is colorful and the fact that His attributes and character are reflected in visual beauty affects our perspective of how to express our worship before Him.

It's almost as though God says, "Wait, not enough color!" Around His throne is a rainbow (see Rev. 4:3). The fading, incomplete rainbows of Earth are show-stopping enough. Who can resist the pull to stare at a rainbow as it forms in the sky after the rain? What must a rainbow in heaven be like? The primary colors of the spectrum are glistening in perfection, each color bleeding into the other as the bands of the rainbow touch each other, resulting in every tint and hue possible. John can only describe it as "resembling an emerald" (Rev. 4:3). Does this mean that the color green is emphasized more than the others, or that its shape is like an emerald? It is unclear. One thing is for certain, though—it is a dazzling sight that enhances the worship experience of heaven.

As we continue to pan away from the throne, we see 24 elders seated on their own thrones (see Rev. 4:4).

Again, there is much insight to be gained here, but our purpose is to note the creative impact of God's worship service. The pageantry of the event is not lost on John, as the elders' golden crowns glisten on their heads. The sight must have been dazzling as they are dressed in white gowns (see Rev. 4:4). Certainly the power of the imagery of purity would be unmistakable, but again, just the sheer impact of so much white would be overwhelming. I am sure that heavenly white robes are the cleanest white that any eye could ever behold. White reflects color, and seeing 24 beings dressed in white while surrounding the colorfulness of God and the rainbow would be a visual overload.

As if this is not enough for the eye gate, God adds lighting to the scene. From the throne there are flashes of lightning (see Rev. 4:5). Having lived in the Midwest of America for a time, I am familiar with lightning. It is blinding. Driving home in the midst of a storm one evening, I saw lightning strike on the highway a couple hundred yards in front of me. I was momentarily blinded and had to pull off the road. For hours, every time I blinked or closed my eyes I would see the flash of light burned into my vision. God has this same light shooting out of His throne—all the time! Flash after flash. The effect would be like that of a strobe light in a hip dance club. God has one in His throne room—amazing!

Lest we think there is enough light, God also has seven lamps blazing. According to the apostle, these are the seven spirits of God (see Rev. 4:5), and there is much speculation as to what this means. Suffice to say, these are not gently burning candles in the corner. They are blazing torches, their flickering illumination mixing with the intensity of the strobe like flashes of light coming from the throne. There is no light show like this in any stadium or concert hall in the world! God rules.

We must not miss the audio department. Along with the lightning are great rumblings and peals of thunder. Again, thinking back to my experiences in the Midwest, I can remember times when the thunder would rumble in the air, almost unceasingly creating an eerie sense of power, making me feel very small and at the mercy of whatever the storm would unleash. Every once and a while a clap of thunder would snap so close by that the entire house would shake with its power. This is happening right in the throne room. The vibrations from subwoofers can be enough to unsettle the bones and vibrate the chest at certain volumes (much to the chagrin of some church elders—doesn't seem to bother the elders in heaven though!) and this cannot come close to the intensity of thunder. If one were to run around heaven with a decibel meter trying to figure out the appropriate volume for worship, it would be a futile undertaking.

This is not the only sound, however. There are the voices of living creatures (we'll get to them in a moment) that keep saying, "Holy, holy, holy is the Lord God Almighty, who was, and is, and is to come" (Rev. 4:8). It is an unceasing refrain. It goes on day and night, night and day. In the midst of this unceasing proclamation, these same creatures also break into expressions of glory, honor and thanks (see Rev. 4:9). This eruption of praise has a sense of spontaneity about it that is so moving that it compels the elders to cast down their crowns before the throne (see Rev. 4:10). It is unclear how this all works together, but the image seems to be of an unbroken flow of worship that swells into various expressions of song centered on the theme of God's holiness. But John's words cannot fully describe all that he is taking in, since human language falls short of capturing heaven's dynamics.

In the midst of all this praise, I cannot help but notice the four living creatures. Deep in the creative genius of God, these beings were envisioned and given life in order to stand around His throne in front of the elders, forever giving Him worship. They are quite remarkable, and unlike anything we have ever seen. I am amazed at the thought that there are beings created by God that are not human, not angelic, but totally distinct from either race. There are at least four of these creatures; they are covered in eyes, front and back (see Rev. 4:6). One is like a lion, one is like an ox, yet another has a face like a man, and the last is like a flying eagle (see Rev. 4:7). Each one has six wings, and each wing is once again covered with eyes—and John is careful to note that even underneath the wings there are more eyes (see Rev. 4:8).

I have had many people tell me of those great believers whom they can hardly wait to meet on the other side. Moses, David and Isaiah are among those who are commonly mentioned. I'm not so sure why, but I am absolutely intrigued by these creatures around the throne; and besides seeing the face of my Savior, I can hardly wait to go and spend some time with these awesome beings. I've been around humans my whole life—I can't wait to spend time with these four beings. What will it be like to look into those eyes? God is too amazing!

In front of this whole extravaganza, God reproduces the image again and again with crystal-clear clarity by throwing a mirror in front of everything. All John can say is that he sees "what looked like a sea of glass, clear as crystal" before the throne (Rev. 4:6). Imagine a still lake that reflects its surrounding landscape from a distance, doubling the image. If we were to step closer and look straight into its depths, we would see it duplicated over and over. So, too, God mirrors the image, creating an unending display of His throne, lightning, creatures, elders, rainbows— a sight that must be indescribable.

Here we see the unmistakable truth that God delights in a multisensory expression of praise before Him. The power of creativity that is expressed here causes the elders to declare the worth of God and to assert that He receive all glory and honor and power (see Rev. 4:11). The reason for this outburst is because God has "created all things" (Rev. 4:11)—and it is for His pleasure that they have been created. Creativity inspires praise.

For communities that have been awakened by the redeeming power of Jesus, one of the greatest aspects of what has been restored to us is the power of the arts. Of all the vehicles for artistic exploration on the planet, the Church should be its foremost patron and protector. We have much to relearn about the Church becoming a safe place for the arts to flourish again.

Remedying the Church's Neglect of the Arts

In both my cross-denominational and international journeys, one of the most broken groups of people that I encounter are artists. Somehow, particularly in evangelical brands of Christianity, they have been lost in the shuffle, and the Church has lost its way when it comes to encouraging gifted artists. Many of them are out in the marketplace and performing on the world's stage—but with very little understanding and support from the Church. I might point out here that embracing creativity and the arts by providing a safe atmosphere in church community for them to be explored and supported is a significant part of our effectiveness in being salt and light to the world around us. There is much to be discussed and wrestled through on this topic, and this treatise will not suffice in addressing the issue; but we should take note of and ponder these issues as we seek to unlock the worship God seeks in our communities.

We are not only talking about tagging on a skit to the end of a worship set or waving a few flags. These things can be a good starting place, but what God is seeking is a creative expression before His throne that is filled with passion and life, spilling out of the box we call church and impacting the world around us with passion and excellence.

The modern Christian world and what is known as evangelicalism in general is marked, in the area of the arts and cultural endeavor, by one outstanding feature, and that is its addiction to mediocrity.

This has borne bitter, bitter fruit—by the stifling and destroying of God-given creative instincts in individuals, the false guilt feelings of those with creative talents in a church which looks at them askance as somehow dabbling in an unspiritual sphere of life. This has produced the unhappy lack of enjoyment of the world around us, God's creativity, man's creativity and the fullness of what we are supposedly redeemed to in Christ, and of course the bitter fruit of having contributed heavily through this unhappy view of the arts to the erosion of the Christian consensus.

Any group that willingly or unconsciously sidesteps creativity and human experience gives up their effective role in the society in which they live. In Christian terms, their ability to be the salt of that society is greatly diminished.[3]

Following the Lead of the Creator

The resurrected Jesus walks into one of the early churches, a growing community in Laodicea. They seem to have it all, and for all intents and purposes is a very successful church. Yet Christ has something against them.

It is important to note how Jesus defines Himself as He speaks to this church. He comes to them as the Amen, steady and unchangeable in His purpose and His promise; and as the faithful and true witness, One who speaks with only truth, who is to be trusted and believed; and as *the beginning of the creation of God* (see Rev. 3:14).

He is speaking from the perspective of an artist. However, not some melancholic, emotionally charged artiste—He is the Amen, the faithful and true witness—

but as the purest creative Being in the universe, the One from whom all ability to create and all creativity spring. Another appropriate translation of the text would be to state that Jesus here is described as the source of God's creation. As the Creator, and as the One from whom all creativity comes, He has an opinion regarding the activity of this church.

He hates it.

Just as lukewarm water is too tepid to be a satisfying drink and too weak to provide a soothing bath, so the deeds of this church are useless, flat and uninspiring. Jesus longs to receive the activities of the church—their gatherings, their liturgy, their acts of service, their lives before Him—yet they are neither hot nor cold, but lukewarm. And He will spit them out of His mouth (see Rev. 3:15-16).

Just as a passionless expression is distasteful to us, so, too, it is to God. To keep our focus on the theme of worship, liturgy that is not "hot" enough to soothe the aching soul—like a soothing soak in a hot spring for the body—is spit out of the mouth. And liturgy that is not "cold" enough to refresh the dry and arid heart—like a cold, refreshing drink of water on a hot day—is spit out of the mouth.

Creating a Passionate Worship

Passionate worship requires some skill, not in some elitist way, but because we put our all into expressing this worship to God. It is not a practice focused on winning a competition or the next Dove Award; rather, it springs from a desire to give God our best and to pour out our all before Him. Such worship refuses to be drawn from the well of lukewarmness but seeks to overflow with passion and life.

All of Christian worship should be marked by such passion, such vitality. God is alive. Jesus has conquered death. The Holy Spirit is not a force to be manipulated by the whims and incantations of liturgy; rather, He is God—the One who sovereignly leads the worship of the saints. We no longer bring the sacrifices of dead animals or the blood appeasement by which there is no lasting forgiveness of sin; but rather we come sprinkled clean by a Blood that speaks a better word than the blood of Abel, and we abandon ourselves before God's throne as living sacrifices. Our songs do not just move within the confines of our notes and scales, but they also become a melody of life whereby everything we do now brings glory to God. Even our eating and drinking become expressions of praise as we live and move and have our being in Him (see Acts 17:28).

Such creativity, freedom and life surely cannot be contained in just one or two songs. Such worship cannot be fully expressed in just one liturgy or style of music. Such praise cannot be displayed through just one language or cultural perspective. No. From the vantage point of God's eternal throne, we can see a symphony of worship and adoration coming before Him from every tongue, tribe and nation. There are sounds and chants; dances and rhythms; melodies and tunes being released across the spectrum of the nations and denominations, and weaving in and out of each other to reach God's ear for His delight and pleasure. From our small corner of the world and the Church, we add our sound to the surging sounds of praise around the world, not able to see or hear the whole. Yet God sees and hears it all.

God designed worship to come to Him from every thing He created. The angels worship. The elders fall before Him. The living beasts (remember the eyes!) give glory, honor and thanks. Mankind, the redeemed crown of God's creation, joins in the song. If we, His people, do not give Him glory, the very rocks of the earth would do so. This worship cannot be contained. This worship is unstoppable.

Sing joyfully to the LORD, you righteous; it is fitting for the upright to praise him. Praise the LORD with the harp; make music to him on the ten-stringed lyre. Sing to him a new song; play skillfully, and shout for joy. For the word of the LORD is right and true; he is faithful in all he does. The LORD loves righteousness and justice; the earth is full of his unfailing love. By the word of the LORD were the heavens made, their starry host by the breath of his mouth. He gathers the waters of the sea into jars; he puts the deep into storehouses. Let all the earth fear the LORD; let all the people of the world revere him. For he spoke, and it came to be; he commanded, and it stood firm. The LORD foils the plans of the nations; he thwarts the purposes of the peoples. But the plans of the LORD stand firm forever, the purposes of his heart through all generations. Blessed is the nation whose God is the LORD, the people he chose for his inheritance. From the heaven the LORD looks down and sees all [humankind]; from his dwelling place he watches all who live on earth—he who forms the hearts of all, who considers everything they do. No king is saved by the size of his army; no warrior escapes by his great strength. A horse is a vain hope for deliverance; despite all its great strength it cannot save. But the eyes of the LORD are on those who fear him, on those whose hope is in his unfailing love, to deliver them from death and keep them alive in famine. We wait in hope for the LORD; he is our help and our shield. In him our hearts rejoice, for we trust in his holy name. May your unfailing love rest upon us, O LORD, even as we put our hope in you (Ps. 33).

All the Nations of the Earth

God's desire is for the full spectrum of worship to represent every tongue, every tribe and every nation. The place of Zion is a place for all peoples (see Ps. 87). The house of prayer is a place of access before God for all nations (see Isa. 56).

This is expressed nowhere more powerfully than through the prophet Isaiah in chapter 56, as God unveils His heart for the nations.

And the Foreigners, Too

God says the foreigners will come (see Isa. 56:6-8). They will come from cultures unlike ours. They will come speaking languages we do not understand. They will express their hearts before heaven in ways that will stretch us. There must be an atmosphere of acceptance, and in the place of worship we must make room for those unlike us: "Let no foreigner who has bound himself to the LORD say, 'The LORD will surely exclude me from his people'" (Isa. 56:3).

How many times have we—particularly those of us from Western cultures—told the foreigners that they are unacceptable here? We have walked into places on the earth again and again and have told people that they are not received by God as they are. We have told people of other languages that their language was spawned from a demonic source because it was not our own. We have told countless tribes that their regalia and expression of the heart could not be turned toward God, for He only heard the liturgies and hymns of the West. We convinced people group after people group that the highest form of worship expression before heaven was our own. We forced our songs to be translated, our customs to be copied, our suits to be envied and our approaches to church life imitated over and over again. God must be grieved, for many reasons, not the least of which that much of the creativity and breadth of worship has been stolen from Him in our shortsightedness and religiosity. Tragic.

> And foreigners who bind themselves to the LORD to serve him, to love the name of the LORD, and to worship him, all who keep the Sabbath without desecrating it and who hold fast to my covenant—these I will bring to my holy mountain and give them joy in my house of prayer. Their burnt offerings and sacrifices will be accepted on my altar; for my house will be called a house of prayer for all nations (Isa. 56:6-7).

A House of Prayer Inhabited by All the Nations

I will never forget the grace and beauty of the tea garden dancers. Their motion in tandem with the sounds of the tabla drums and Himalayan flutes moved something deep within me. This was worship. And yet somehow, they weren't quite sure this was true. This was to be a presentation to honor their friend from the West, and now he was to come forward and teach them about worship. As I walked forward, still greatly impacted by what I had seen and felt, I was aware that the Holy Spirit was resisting me in my planned talk for the evening. I sensed that God was delighted with the sounds and movement that had just taken place and that I was to make the people aware of His delight.

We turned to Isaiah 56, and I explained to the crowd gathered that their sounds, their dance, their language were acceptable before God—and that they didn't need to use only Western music and Western approaches to worship. There was a deep pondering that happened as many of them did not really believe that this was true. Despite all the good that the Western Church had brought, the influence of our culture had smothered their own and had relegated it to pagan at best, demonic at worst.

I called the tabla player back to the front and encouraged him on his skill and playing ability. I told him that his playing was not just for Nepali cultural gatherings and for the tourists from other places; rather, this sound needed to be present around the throne of God as He called for worship from every tongue and tribe. We began to pray, and he began to play. Slowly a sound began to emerge as other instruments joined in, and the people began to sing in their own language—and from a place in their hearts that was truly their own, not filtered through a Western lens.

It is very hard to worship in spirit and truth (as we discussed earlier) if we are not able to use our own language, our own rhythms and our own culture. A freedom that was contagious began to stir in the room and from all I could see the Holy Spirit sustained it. For many there, this was the first time they had expressed authentic worship.

There was a resonance unlike any I had witnessed before. I was hearing tonal scales that I'd never heard before. There were approaches to rhythm and harmony that my ear was unaccustomed to. A purer sound of worship I had rarely heard. I did not lead one song and did not give any direction from the moment the tabla player began to play. I sat down—I was in awe of what was taking place. As I watched the Holy Spirit lead worship, my understanding of the worship God seeks was stretched again. They continued for hours and hours, long after I left. I am told that things finally settled down at about 2 A.M., five to six hours after we had begun.

I am in no way a syncretist. Idolatry must be purged from the heart of all expressions of worship, but we must not be so quick to call cultural expression idolatry. A particular culture in and of itself is not evil. There is much that we assume is acceptable in worship because we are comfortable with it; and since we are so inclined, we deem it to be acceptable before God.

This is not simply about multiculturalism either. It is about discovering the culture of the kingdom of heaven, and under the rule and reign of God allowing for the fullest release of worship possible.

Our challenge in this regard is not just relegated to cross-cultural issues. There are also intergenerational and interdenominational hurdles to be navigated. There is not enough room here to delve into all the implications, but once again I invite you to wrestle with what the acceptance of the foreigner means in your liturgical, political, social and economic setting.

God is seeking a worship that reflects His heart. As the truly original artist, He delights in worship that echoes the creativity and passion that He put into creation. He longs for worship that reflects not only the expanse of creation but also the fullest expression of His crown of creation: redeemed humanity worshipping Him from every tongue, tribe and nation. We need to cultivate creativity and artistic expression in our worship, not to impress God, or put our talents on display before Him, but simply because He enjoys it. This is the worship He seeks.

Chapter Six

LET **JUSTICE ROLL**

*As the Body of Christ, we are to continue
the mission of the Incarnate One in the world
today and that includes an ongoing offensive
against the fallen principalities and powers,
a vigorous, active use of power in the search
for greater justice in society.*

—RONALD J. SIDER, QUOTED IN *ANNOUNCING THE KINGDOM:
THE STORY OF GOD'S MISSION IN THE BIBLE*

Some days I find myself actually aching to see the return of Christ. Caught in the time between the times, having tasted of a measure of the Kingdom's breakthrough, I still long for more, knowing that its fullness will be in eternity. I groan.

This angst penetrates my worship, as intercession bleeds into my song, and my life of worship becomes intertwined with the poor, the marginalized and the oppressed. It would seem that the expression of worship this side of heaven will always be touched by brokenness and a longing for things to be set right. To ignore this is to gut worship of its authenticity, and to create something that God is not pleased with.

THE NATURE OF WORSHIP: CENTERED ON CHRIST

Lying at the heart of worship is tension. Seeing Jesus in the midst of brokenness. Finding His glory in the place of weakness and suffering.

> In putting everything under him, God left nothing that is not subject to him. Yet at present we do not see everything subject to him. But we see Jesus (Heb. 2:8-9).

In our present struggles, both personal as well as those engulfing the peoples of the earth, we must have a vision of Christ. Worship is not an escape. It is perspective. What or whom we worship shapes our worldview, and it is from this vantage point that we see the people and the world around us. Theology is critical. We cannot fully know God without seeing Him as revealed in Christ. We must see Jesus.

Jesus Came to Draw His People Close to Him

Jesus is "the image of the invisible God, the firstborn over all creation" (Col. 1:15). He is the One whom the prophets spoke of and longed to know. The final prophet in the Old Testament tradition, the eccentric Baptist, spoke straight out the heart of Isaiah's foresight, becoming the voice in the wilderness preparing the way of the Lord—this Jesus (see Matt. 3:1-3).

Comfort, comfort my people, says your God. Speak tenderly to Jerusalem, and proclaim to her that her hard service has been completed, that her sin has been paid for, that she has received from the LORD's hand double for all her sins. *A voice of one calling: "In the desert prepare the way for the LORD; make straight in the wilderness a highway for our God.* Every valley shall be raised up, every mountain and hill made low; the rough ground shall become level, the rugged places a plain" (Isa. 40:1-4, emphasis added).

This good news was to be fleshed out before all humankind. The mists of prophetic vision were about to clear and its fulfillment come. The time had arrived for God to show Himself.

And the glory of the LORD will be revealed, and all [humankind] together will see it (Isa. 40:5).

Jesus' Glory Is Revealed in Love

We long for revealed glory. If God would just come down; if His presence would come in such a way that revival swept the land as an unstoppable force; then everything would be OK. This is our hope in the worship encounter. We cry out, "Let Your glory fall!"

Yet how does He reveal Himself? I am sure that the prophets expected their words to be fulfilled in fiery splendor. Hadn't Isaiah already witnessed the Lord's train filling the Temple in such an overwhelming display of power that it left him completely undone? (See Isa. 6). I am sure that the Jews expected chariots and angels, thunder and storm. I have felt many times the expectancy in the midst of gathered worship that at any moment the ceiling would split open and the glory of God would be revealed. Never do I imagine it as a tame entrance. At times I am sure that this is true.

But still, we see Jesus . . .

Who has believed our message and to whom has the arm of the LORD been revealed? He grew up before him like a tender shoot, and like a root out of dry ground. He had no beauty or majesty to attract us to him, nothing in his appearance that we should desire him. He was despised and rejected by [people], a man of sorrows, and familiar with suffering. Like one from whom [people] hide their faces he was despised, and we esteemed him not. Surely he took up our infirmities and carried our sorrows, yet we considered him stricken by God, smitten by him, and afflicted. But he was pierced for our transgressions, he was crushed for our iniquities; the punishment that brought us peace was upon him, and by his wounds we are healed. We all, like sheep, have gone astray, each of us has turned to his [or her] own way; and the LORD has laid on him the iniquity of us all (Isa. 53:1-6).

We love these passages, and we meditate on them each year as Holy Week comes round. But what we often fail to see is that, within their literary context, they form the climax of that great sustained passage of prophecy which purports to speak of how the living God returns to woo and win his people. What will it look like when God comes back to Jerusalem? Isaiah's answer is that it will not be a blaze of glory. It will not be in the form of a great military display of power. It will be in the life of One who takes upon Himself the form of a servant, and is obedient to death. . . . To a world besotted with the love of power, Isaiah's God reveals himself in the power of love.[1]

N. T. Wright's words strike at the heart of the matter. Just as the Hebrews could not conceive of the Messiah being anything like Jesus (in fact, they saw Christ as a blasphemer), so we also, at times, misunderstand how God comes. We long for acts of power, and yet God may be revealing Himself through a simple act of kindness. We long for a display of glory that is all lights and glitz that rock the room, and yet God may be revealing Himself through a compassionate embracing of the poor. We long for an expression of worship that blows us away in an overwhelming display of God's presence, and yet God may be revealing Himself by challenging the injustice around us and caring for those it has abused.

The power of this love is far from soppy sentimentalism. This is a love that moves. This is a love that cannot stand still. The comfort this love brings moves into the darkest chambers of oppression. It touches the sick and the broken. It is a love that is not afraid of sorrow, pain and poverty. It is born of the Spirit, revealing the heart of the Father.

> The Spirit of the Sovereign LORD is on me, because the LORD has anointed me to preach good news to the poor. He has sent me to bind up the brokenhearted, to proclaim freedom for the captives and release from darkness for the prisoners, to proclaim the year of the LORD's favor (Isa. 61:1-2).

Our worship must move us to this kind of love if it is to be authentic and Christ centered.

> Paul summarized this call to the violence of love by encouraging the church not to be overcome by evil, through playing evil's game by using the world's weaponry of necessity. Rather, the church is to "overcome evil with good" (Romans 12:14-21). Of course, the church is to serve as the advocate of the poor and the oppressed and is to challenge all injustice in society.[2]

At the roots of injustice is the abuse of power. Whether it is a parent to a child, a peace officer to a suspect, a doctor to a patient, a ruler to a nation, where there is an abuse of power there is injustice. God, who holds all authority and all power, is never abusive; and as the source of all authority and power, He is deeply grieved to witness injustice throughout all of His creation. He administers His justice from the position of love, for He is love.

The advent message, Isaiah's message for his hearers, is that his God is coming to judge the world by the law of love. There is always a danger that when we speak of God's judgment we imagine God as a fierce, bullying, domineering God. I suspect that many people in our society today, if they use the word "God" at all (other than just an expletive), think of God basically like that. . . . There are quite enough fierce bullies in the world already without having one up in the sky as well. But the reason the true God will come to right all wrongs in the world (and that's what "judgment" really means) is not because he is a fierce bully but precisely because he is the bridegroom who wants to woo and win his bride.[3]

One of the most enduring artistic works of worship in human history comes from Isaiah's prophecy. It is Handel's composition *Messiah*. Apart from the speed with which it was written and its melodic capturing of the advent themes of Isaiah that we have been wrestling with here, there is another striking feature of this lasting work. Almost every performance of *Messiah* while Handel was alive was done for charity—and even upon his death he had the masterpiece willed to a hospital.

In the fall of 1741, his finances again stretched perilously thin, Handel accepted a job offer in Dublin. (His Irish sojourn is a factual nugget key to Devine Entertainment's "Handel's Last Chance.") He came with *The Messiah* in hand, a spectacular oratorio he had written in a mere three weeks that August, an astonishing pace even for a man who was famous for composing quickly. After extensive rehearsals, it debuted on April 13, 1742 at a charity performance—*during his lifetime, he almost invariably had it performed for charity*—in front of a standing-room-only audience at Dublin's New Music Hall.

Though he had no children of his own—Handel died a confirmed bachelor—he cared greatly for the disadvantaged young, and thus in his will left *The Messiah*, arguably his greatest work, to London's Foundling Hospital.[4]

Upon completing the "Hallelujah Chorus," Handel would say, "I did think I did see all Heaven before me, and the great God Himself."[5] Could it be, that in seeing God he saw this King of Justice, this suffering servant King, and to separate the performance of the *Messiah* from tangible acts of love and charity would be impossible?

As odd as it may seem, far from the gathered place of praise, we often discover worship among the poor and the broken. Until Christ returns again, glory and sorrow will not be separated. There is a day coming when every tear will be wiped away, and all sorrow, disease and pain be banished forever. We celebrate its coming and live in the perspective that it brings. But for now, our worship is meshed with sorrow—not just our own but also that of the world around us.

THE INTERCESSORY ASPECT OF WORSHIP

We have already addressed the need for the lament in our worship, and the reality that there is no "truth" in "spirit and truth" apart from a deep and honest heart cry woven into our expression of worship. This is not only personal, however. Worship and intercession flow together, and we cannot lose the intensity of this in our liturgies. To cry out on behalf of local, national and international issues of brokenness within our worship is acceptable. In fact, the most common word for prayer in the Scriptures is the Hebrew term *tepillah*. It means "a prayer set to music and sung in formal worship."[6] It is the type of prayer in the house for all nations (see Isa. 56:7), Habakkuk's prayer and Hannah's prayer (see 1 Sam. 2:1-10), and describes all the Psalms, or "prayers" of Psalms 1 through 72.

Praying for Justice

The intercessory cry for justice expressed through our music and liturgy keeps our gatherings grounded—and something that the Lord invites and delights in. Just as Jesus is our great intercessor, so we position ourselves before the throne on behalf of others—a cry for the salvation of the least, the last and the lost. The issues of war; AIDS; poverty; urban struggles; and the plight of the immigrant, orphans and widows must be allowed to bleed into our worship as worship and intercession embrace and move us to compassionate acts in the name of Christ.

This posture of intercession and worship is critical for the Church, for our wrestle is not simply against flesh and blood. The enemy of justice is not only initiated by human brokenness and natural forces but is also a web of satanic and demonic deceit that seeps into every system and institution known on the earth.

The New Testament and the record of church history bear ample witness to the fact that despite the cross and the nullification of the real threat of the powers, they still dominate all people to a greater or lesser degree. They relentlessly attack the church and seek by every means to hinder the church's missionary obedience. Their abode remains in the "heavenly realms" surrounding the visible world (Eph. 3:10). From there they venture forth to menace, seduce, and in other ways thwart the ongoing movement of the Kingdom of God among the nations. Often they do this through incarnating themselves in existing structures in society and in cultural traditions and religious institutions. On occasion, however, they assault individuals directly.[7]

Praying for the Salvation of All Who Dwell on the Earth

As we draw near to God in worship, the surrounding darkness becomes more evident. As we align ourselves under the reign of Christ in worship, the stark difference between the systems of the world, the kingdom of darkness and God's kingdom of light is glaringly obvious. We have tasted of freedom and the salvation that the Kingdom brings. We cannot remain silent concerning the plight of those still living under the oppression of the dark kingdom and its weight of injustice. Our worship does not isolate us; rather, as we draw near to God's heart, we are stirred by His longing to see salvation visit the whole earth and to shatter the works of Satan.

To understand salvation biblically, it's important that it be described in broader terms than that which a self-absorbed evangelicalism allows. The biblical perspective is very holistic and encompasses all of life. Salvation is intertwined with the Hebrew understanding of "shalom"—peace in all of life. While the emphasis on the spiritual truth of salvation is paramount, it is not to be divorced from that of a wider application.

> The OT usage of the term to express God's action in saving his people from their enemies has been taken as normative, and salvation has been understood as freeing people from hunger, poverty and the threat of war so that they may live a whole life in the world.[8]

The salvation that the kingdom of God brings and conversely the worship that resonates at its heart is not dualistic. Both penetrate all of life. Jesus fully embraced what it meant to be human, and for Him this was not piety that was divorced from temptation and suffering. His perfection was not attained by a kind of holy separation from the realities of oppression and suffering in the world; rather, it was maintained as He was moved by compassion into the harassment and helplessness of those around him. Indeed, even Jesus learned obedience through suffering, and in doing so He became the perfect mediator between God and humanity (see Heb. 5:8-9).

When we strip away the activities of justice from the life of worship, we stray from God's intent for His kingdom people. Righteousness and justice are the very foundations of His throne (see Ps. 89:14). To be holy is to be just; under this Kingdom reign, to love God and to love one's neighbor are synonymous.

English translates this semantic field with two different roots: "right," "righteous," and "righteousness" and "just," "justice," "justify," and "justification." In Hebrew and Greek, however, *these ideas all belong together linguistically and theologically.*[9]

God rules from a "throne of grace" (Heb. 4:16) that is established on righteousness and justice. The law of the land is the law of love. In this kingdom, justice is administered out of mercy. There is freedom for both the oppressed and the oppressor. There is hope for all to be transformed as we submit to the King and allow His kingdom to break through. The justice of God is not about human rights and the creation of a human utopia; it is about bringing all things into alignment under the rule and reign of God. It is in this place of surrender and trust that all things find their fullest and most complete expression. The Kingdom reign is a just one with God its center.

> Here is my servant, whom I uphold, my chosen one in whom I delight; I will put my Spirit on him and he will bring justice to the nations. He will not shout or cry out, or raise His voice in the streets. A bruised reed he will not break, and a smoldering wick he will not snuff out. In faithfulness he will bring forth justice; he will not falter or be discouraged till he establishes justice on earth (Isa. 42:1-4).

From God's kingdom perspective, and because of His very nature—God is love—to bring worship before Him that is not anchored to mercy and justice is incomplete, and something that He cannot accept. Worship given to God must reflect God's character. He is King and rules over all the earth, and His people must reflect His reign on the earth. To relegate His rule to a weekly meeting contained in a structure made with human hands and a programmatic life divorced from the needs of the society in which it exists is to miss the breadth of the impact of His reign and the worship that it demands.

To see God's invasion of grace into our lives as something that is "just" for us—which results in the creation of Christian ghettos and a detachment from the world's issues—is tragic. Only the Church, the continuing incarnation of Jesus on the earth, can step into shattered society and bring an alternate community that truly breaks the back of injustice. It is only a Spirit-breathed community that can take people past charity, programs and welfare into a life of freedom and salvation.

Christians in the world have a role to fill that non-Christians cannot possibly fill. They have to break the fatality that hangs over the world through reflecting in every way the victory that Christ gained over the powers. They are to be a sign of the new covenant, a demonstration that a new order has entered the world, giving meaning, direction, and hope to history.[10]

As we touch the oppressed and marginalized with tangible acts of love, it moves God. As sure as a cup of cold water eases the thirst of parched lips—whether on the streets of Los Angeles or in the searing heat of the Sudan—it touches the very lips of God. Jesus said it this way, "Whatever you did for one of the least of these brothers [and sisters] of mine, you did for me" (Matt. 25:40).

When we capture God's heart for the poor and broken (as James 2 tells us, the poor in the eyes of the world—not a spiritualized poverty among suburbanites) it begins to move us to action, it is worship. This King longs to move from His throne and end all injustice forever. His wrath is kindled against unrighteousness (remember, that is actually injustice); and He wants to unlock the time when His Anointed One returns to establish His reign of peace forever.

Yet He waits. It is not slowness like the lethargic inactivity of a human being, but it is the patience of a God of love who holds back ultimate justice to give room for more people to choose to follow Him. The climactic establishment and final culmination of His kingdom reign through the return of Christ will be final. There will be no more choice after that moment. And so He waits. A day. A thousand years. A thousand years. A day. Time is not the issue; the patient heart of God is the focus here—one more day to see more people enter His kingdom and His rest.

This tears at the very fabric of God's being, for one more day means one more day of war, disease, famine, abuse and injustice. So as He waits, we walk into the midst of a hurting world, just as Jesus did, and administer acts of justice springing from love and mercy. It is then that worship becomes sweet. The songs ring true.

The church is to be not only an example of God's intended new humanity, but the means by which the eventual plan, including the establishment of world-wide justice, is to be put into effect.[11]

The prophet Amos captures the heart of God regarding this matter.

> I hate, I despise your religious feasts; I cannot stand your assemblies. Even though you bring me burnt offerings and grain offerings, I will not accept them. Though you bring choice fellowship offerings, I will have no regard for them. Away with the noise of your songs! I will not listen to the music of your harps. But let justice roll on like a river, righ-teousness like a never-failing stream! (Amos 5:21-24).

Even though the choicest of fellowship offerings were brought before Him, something was missing. What was to be a fragrant offering before heaven had become something much less, a sacrifice He could not receive. Our acts of worship divorced from a lifestyle of mercy and justice create the same effect. The liturgy must stop. The music must be quieted. (I haven't seen a Christian bumper sticker made of these verses yet!) God cannot receive the worship of His people until "justice roll[s] on like a river, [and] righteousness like a never-failing stream" (v. 24).

LET JUSTICE ROLL—A LESSON
IN CHURCH HISTORY

Until the early 1900s, evangelism and social action had never been divorced from one another. The Puritan dream had been of a new Israel. America was the land of destiny; and men like Finney believed with all their hearts that through salvation, men and women could make the world a better place in which to live. The mandate "Be perfect, therefore, as your heavenly Father is perfect" (Matt. 5:48) was not only doable but necessary. Christians were to be involved in social action as a demonstration of the genuineness of their faith. After all, it was James himself who said, "Faith without works is dead" (see Jas. 2:26).

However, by the end of the First World War, there was a roaring controversy in the American Church between the Fundamentalists and the Modernists. The Fundamentalists wanted to hold to the message of historic Christianity and the uniqueness of Christ. The Modernists wanted to promote a new understanding of Christianity as one among many valid religions. But something else was happening. The Fundamentalists lost a lot of their battles in the mainline denominations and either were kicked out or left in a huff. The Modernists held on to the institutions and a lot of the old money. With this money they funded their "social gospel" projects. The Fundamentalists had to start over, and understandably, they concentrated on the core message that they thought the Modernists had forsaken. Church historian David Moberg has called this "the great reversal"[12] because both sides of the controversy retreated from the wholistic message of the gospel, which addresses both spiritual and social realities.

LET WORSHIP AND JUSTICE KISS

It is my conviction that we must regain the fusion of worship and justice. A prudent question for us today would be, Is God even listening? "Away with the

The fragrance of worship is justice—where there is no justice, there is no fragrance.

noise of your songs" is the last thing the worshipping church wants to hear from heaven, but do we have courage to listen if that is what God is telling us?

I clearly remember being struck with this thought: *The fragrance of worship is justice—where there is no justice, there is no fragrance.* I'm not quite sure how the thought came, but I am forever grateful for the journey that it sent my family and me on. This awareness came to me by the grace of God before I had any songs published or had any kind of exposure to the Church at large through the avenue of worship music. I do not exaggerate to say that I thank God almost every day for giving me this perspective of a worshipper's life. As we have worked in various communities planting churches and trying to cultivate space for followers of Christ to gather, we have always tried to build resting on this foundation.

Our mission has never been about big programs or thinking we could fix all the issues of injustice in the world. It has simply been about worship and compassion. If God's ability to receive our worship was connected to our attitudes and heart posture toward the poor and the unjustly afflicted, we had to set our life's course on wrestling with what that meant. If the center of the Kingdom was found on the fringes of the world's systems, then we wanted to dwell there. If Jesus was to be discovered in special ways amongst the broken and disenfranchised, then that is where we wanted to be. There is a sound that comes from dwelling here that cannot be unlocked any other place. There is a fragrance released from amongst the least of which there is no equal to outside of heaven.

So we began with simplicity, and have tried to maintain that stance as we have explored the correlation between worship and justice. It has taken us from acts such as giving a blanket out of our own closet to an old, abandoned woman in a motel to planting a church in a broken urban environment in the heart of a city. It has taken us to friendship with people far out of our comfort zone and into an encounter with Jesus.

A FINAL THOUGHT: THE IMPORTANCE OF COMMUNITY

One more thing must be noted here. We can only live out justice if we are part of a worshipping community, connected with other people. The journey into the worship God seeks is one that takes us into community. For the most part, we have focused on the expression of justice beyond the bounds of the infrastructure of the local Church. It would be wrong, however, not to mention the need for relational justice to be at the very heart of the local church as well.

> Therefore, if you are offering your gift at the
> altar and there remember that your brother
> [or sister] has something against you, leave
> your gift at the altar. First go and be recon-
> ciled to your brother [sister]; then come and
> offer your gift (Matt. 5:23-24).

We are to be marked by love, and it is only in such a place that the bonds of injustice and the abuse of power can truly be broken. It is by our love that the world will know that we are disciples of Christ. It is by our love that our worship is marked as acceptable before the King of love Himself.

It is time for the Church to recover the worship that has love at its core. Love for God that is expressed through love for our neighbor. The worship that God is seeking is a worship that is rooted in love for each other. To be a righteous people is to be a just people. To be a worshipping people is to see at the heart of community the glory of justice breaking into a world of injustice.

Yet at present we do not see everything subject to Him.

But we see Jesus.

Chapter Seven

THE JOURNEY FROM HERE

We can't just acknowledge a God like this at a distance, and carry on as before.

—N. T. WRIGHT,
*FOR ALL GOD'S WORTH: TRUE WORSHIP
AND THE CALLING OF THE CHURCH*

I feel like I have said so much in this book and yet haven't really said much at all. Maybe this is how most people feel after putting their thoughts into words. I have been trying to explore with you a perspective on worship from God's vantage point; but I know that I have fallen far short of covering everything that is relevant. Perhaps you have more questions now than answers. Maybe that's not so bad.

THE PRICE OF TRUE WORSHIP

Whether we gather to worship in someone's home, in a contemporary megachurch or in a traditional, liturgical setting, there are some specific principles that can help us set our compass toward the worship He desires. As we work toward building a community whose worship delights God, these principles can be applied in any liturgical setting within the wide spectrum of Church subculture. (In fact, these principles are especially critical in a "seeker sensitive" context of helping newcomers encounter the living God, not just our songs or our presentation.)

Take note however: Worship does have a price. I am not talking of sacrifice in the usual mystical sense. I trust that the previous pages have made it clear there is nothing to be done beyond the work of

Christ in regard to our worship. I am speaking of the literal implications of stepping toward a passionate and tangible expression.

You may remember the story of Mary in Mark 14. In the week before His crucifixion, Jesus was enjoying a meal with some close friends when a woman approached him. She was not a stranger to the group; in fact, most scholars are in agreement that this was Mary of Bethany (not to be confused with the "sinful woman" in Luke 7, a powerful story in its own right). Mary of Bethany was the sister of Martha and Lazarus. She so loved Jesus that in the middle of the meal, she could not contain her devotion any longer. The normally quiet Mary shattered the top of an expensive jar of perfume, most likely imported from India, and representing a year's wages to be used as a dowry one day. When she poured it on Jesus' head, it spilled over his whole body.[1]

The true meaning of what happened here will never be grasped until it is realized that when Mary was pouring out her perfume, she was also pouring out her heart, filled with genuine religious love, gratitude, and devotion. The vessel in which the perfume was stored generally had a rather long and narrow neck. This bottle could have been opened or even broken at the top in such a manner that the perfume would have trickled out. But that would not have satisfied Mary. So she broke it in such a manner that the ointment came gushing out over Jesus.[2]

"This is kissing the Son."[3] Mary boldly anointed Jesus, "making him her king."[4]

Such extravagant worship always confronts those who see it. To the disciples, Mary's use of the perfume seemed to be such a waste—at the very least it could have been sold, and the proceeds given to feed the poor (see Mark 14:4-5). To them, this would have been a more appropriate use of something so costly, rather than spilling it in an impulsive act of emotion.

Not only did the friends of Jesus judge Mary's worship, but they also judged her character. They saw her as immature and unrestrained in the presence of the Master, and so they tried to instruct her. Jesus directly contradicted their evaluation by saying, "Why are you bothering her? She has done a beautiful thing to me" (Mark 14:6).

Mary's out-in-the-open worship was not easy for the disciples to understand. It is no easier for us today. Tangible expression of worship will cost and stretch our sensibilities.

It will impact our finances. Mary literally "wasted" a year's wages in expressing her worship. To express worship in a tangible way, as a community, especially if music and the arts are valued, will take resources.

It will impact reputation. Mary was severely rebuked for her extravagance. Not everyone will understand this kind of adoration. It will demand time to pastor a community through the challenges and misunderstandings that this can create. It will take time to really think through the theological and practical issues of worship. But a commitment to worship will reap great reward.

It will create tension. Instead of Mary's extravagance, some thought a more spiritual act of worship would have been to give to the poor. Jesus, however, does not pit one act against the other. The acts of adoration and mercy will demand our all. There really is no balance here, just tension.

Mary's devotion and the resulting fragrance that filled the house will forever accompany the proclamation of the gospel. The good news comes at an incredible cost. As a result, the gospel cannot be proclaimed without extravagant worship accompanying it.

HOW TO MOVE TOWARD THE WORSHIP GOD IS SEEKING

Cultivate an Atmosphere of Expectation

It never fails. Whenever I gather with others and there is a expectation of encountering God—whether in a living room or in a stone hut 15,000 feet up in the Himalayan mountains or in a stadium—the worship encounter is always more profound. Even considering the influence of crowd dynamics, charismatic leadership and sociological gathering patterns, *expectation* makes all the difference in how we encounter God. (Maybe it has something to do with faith.)

In other words, whatever our liturgy and the vision that draws us, we must carry a sense of anticipation that we will meet with God when we gather in community. Although this can sound somewhat lofty, it simply means that we call each other into a sense of expectancy. We help each other look beyond the form of liturgy to its heart.

This is best accomplished, in my opinion, through modeling. The posture and attitude of leaders, in particular, will set the tone for any gathering;

what leaders do has more impact than they realize. It may be tempting to use the worship time to chat with people or, even worse, to hold mini staff meetings in the front row or use this time for final sermon preparation. The way leaders engage in the worship experience will send a huge message to the church community about the value and expectation placed on the worship time.

The more awareness all of us have of the One with whom we are meeting—the King—the more awesome the encounter will be. Modeling a high anticipation of encountering the Lord will alleviate some of the challenges in leading a worshipping community. As our expectation to encounter God increases, irritants such as showing up on time and squabbles over the style of music or the length of the musical part of the service will lessen (although these are never fully dispelled). As we embrace the reality that God draws near to us as we draw near to Him (see Jas. 4:8), the pressure to hype something up or give people what they want will fade.

Make Room for Spirit and Truth

God wants something real. Most of the time, we want it, too. But something weird seems to happen when we come together as *the* Church. We change, and it's usually not for the better. Even when we hang around after a formal service or a house meeting, we seem to be more real and honest than when we "worship." Our voices change; our posture shifts; and, dare I say, the pretending begins. It seems to me this ought not to be.

God is seeking those who worship in spirit and truth. In this book we have wrestled with some of what that means; and while we must discover what is appropriate and inappropriate within the context of our particular community, we must at the same time break the back of judgmental attitudes that shut down honest expression.

Encounter with the living God can be quite overwhelming, and there must be room for this collision to find honest expression.

Worship can put us in a very vulnerable position. Encounter with the living God can be quite overwhelming, and there must be room for this collision to find honest expression. Nothing quenches a person's expression of worship more than the feeling that it is unsafe to reveal his or her heart.

There is another side to this equation. Worship is also difficult when people demand that anything goes during the worship time, based on their myopic need to express their hearts to God. There are some things that just aren't helpful, such as a boisterous outburst during the contemplative moment of communion, or getting whacked in the head by a banner-waving enthusiast. Corporate worship is a fascinating meshing of personal and communal experience. Deference is vital, and yet it creates a tension. If we are to unlock something that God will take pleasure in, we must make room for the heart.

Allow Room for Risk

In my opinion, there is no way to work through the first couple of points—"cultivate an atmosphere of expectation" and "make room for spirit and truth"—without an element of risk. Where risk is removed from the experience of worship, all that is left is performance. While I am a firm believer in excellence in our worship, to polish the liturgy to such a fine point that there is no adventure is to lose the essence of what God longs for.

It would seem that the worship God seeks is personal and interactive. In it, there is room for creativity and a measure of spontaneity.

I witnessed one of the best examples of this dynamic at a performance of Cirque du Soleil. The excellence, commitment and preparation of the performers were so superior that I was moved to tears. The timing of their acrobatic moves with the music took my breath away as the live band made slight adjustments in order to flow with the movement of the tumblers and entertainers throughout the performance.

At one point, one of the performers attempted a daring move on the high trapeze. As he launched from his perch high above us and sailed through the air, there was a corporate hush. He missed the bar! But, tumbling into the net below, he never missed a beat. The band continued to loop the progression they were playing, and the entertainer climbed the ladder again. The music crescendoed, and he made the leap, this time with success. The crowd, beside itself with delight, cheered him on. I had never seen anything like it. In the midst of one of the most excellent presentations of any artistic endeavor I had ever witnessed, there was room for risk. There was so much synergy between the musicians and the acrobat that what could have been a disastrous mistake was turned into a triumphant success. Room for risk had been built into the routine, and mistakes were not seen as failure but as a challenge to try again until it came out right. I remember thinking, *This is how gathered church should be!*

Create a Sense of Journey

Worship must flow out of community. One of the greatest needs I see in the local church is for a sense of the *journey together*, not just of pulling off another service. When our liturgy is fractured into 52 separate presentations a year, even when it's anchored to tradition and the Church calendar, it is hard to maintain a sense of adventure and relevance.

Worship is the corporate language of faith for a community. Each community needs song and art that express their stage of the journey—that reflect the current challenges, successes, struggles, joys and issues facing that local church. Besides looking to the future, there is a sense of connection to the past and to the rest of the universal Church. There must be fresh and original material that is solid, not only theologically, but also in terms of present realities in the gathered community. Worship material should come both from without and from within the community itself.

Worship is not static; it should be ever fresh. Songs and liturgy that had meaning in the last decade may not reflect with integrity the current heart-cry of the community. Even more important, they may not reflect what the Holy Spirit is currently emphasizing. Without losing connection to where we've been, we must always look forward to the next steps of our journey together.

Equip the Whole Church for Worship

We spend so little time and energy equipping the church body for worship. I am not talking about training to play instruments or learning the skill of worship leading or even training in the arts (although we have a long way to go in this department). I am talking about equipping the whole church to worship. Most of the training that goes on (if it happens at all) is for the worship team. It is rare to see a community that is equipped in the area of worship.

We teach on evangelism and spiritual gifts and make room for all sorts of aspects of what it means to be a follower of Christ in community, but somehow we expect worship to just "magically" happen when we gather. Of course, as I noted earlier, we disagree about what that experience should and should not be, probably more than we do about other aspects of church life. It's too loud, too soft, too short, too long, too many new songs, too many old songs, the art is distracting or not creative enough.

Time given to instruction about the whys and the hows of worship in community is very important. People *can* learn to embrace sounds and expressions that may be out of their comfort zone. Sometimes all it takes is learning where to sit in the room. Some spots will be louder than others, depending on speaker alignment and other factors, and simply moving to a different location could solve a person's problem with volume. Other times it's a matter of education and gaining an understanding of different genres and approaches to music and the arts. It will always take time, however, and unless we take deliberate action to cultivate worship in our communities, it will not happen.

It is essential to find ways to include everyone in the worship experience, without unduly penalizing the gifted. We are about community, but not in the communist sense that all things must be brought to the lowest common denominator to be acceptable, or even accessible. Total conformity can stifle creative energy in liturgy, and this must be avoided. Also, a self-serving artistic community can create a sense of elitism and a focus on performance that can kill corporate worship. To walk in this place of creative tension demands pastoring and instruction for all involved. Those who carry special creative gifting must cultivate an attitude of servanthood as the rest of the community makes room for the excellence of their craft to be displayed to the glory of God, as well.

Issues of taste, style and presentation will always carry a measure of subjectivity. When we teach on worship, we need to discover how to create a sense of community as we express our worship. Worship is not a concert where we pay for a ticket and come to hear what we want, nor is it a time for the gifted to display their talent; it is a time to encounter God. There are times when our greatest act of worship will be to let go of our preferences in worship and defer to others, rejoicing with those who rejoice, as we allow others to express their hearts.

Provide Resources and Support

The amount of resources we put into the expression of worship will reveal the value we place on it. When I travel to different church facilities, I am amazed to see what a small allocation of resources have been put toward the acoustic, visual and artistic aspects of worship. And yet, if there is any area of church life that is scrutinized and criticized more than this, I have yet to find it.

There are times when our greatest act of worship will be to let go of our preferences in worship and defer to others, rejoicing with those who rejoice, as we allow others to express their hearts.

One of the clearest examples of this is the area of audio reinforcement. Many contentions about sound volume are directly related to the amount of finances put toward proper equipment and its usage. Sometimes it is not volume as much as equalization and which frequencies are boosted in the mix. Everything is critical, from speaker placement to the person running the soundboard.

Church communities with a style of worship that uses sound reinforcement for music and any kind of verbal presentation (preaching included) must recognize that there is a commensurate cost involved and that it is just as important as any other expense within the church. If resources are not allocated in this area of the church, then the expectations and demands put on this area should be severely adjusted.

Another great need for support and allocation of resources is in the area of the music and the arts. This is such a massive topic! I can only pique your interest in understanding the need in this area by saying that if we would give as much attention to the arts as we do to preaching, we would be well ahead of the game.

Create a Safe Place for the Arts

I'll never forget one of our Sunday gatherings as a church community in Winnipeg, Canada. We had several worship teams, and each brought its own unique flavor. At this particular meeting—one of our largest gatherings to date—one of our most adventuresome teams was in charge. The building was full, and a huge spectrum of people was present—visitors, relatives, seekers. This Sunday the team decided to try one of the most experimental worship sets I have ever witnessed, and it was a risk.

Not too long into it, I realized it just wasn't going to work. It was like the proverbial snowball rolling down the hill. Momentum carried the thing, and it seemed unstoppable. There was music, painting and motion. The more disconnected the worship team felt, the more bizarre the experience became. People stood in silence, unclear as to how to connect with the artistic swirl coming at them. All eyes were beginning to look over at me. Everyone, from the worship team to the congregation, seemed to be pleading with their eyes, *Do something!*

I walked to the front and gently wound things down. I looked toward the worship team and then to the people and said something like, "This isn't working, is it?" There was affirmation from everyone. I then greeted visitors and people who may not have been accustomed to our church and explained to them the value we place on expressing our hearts before God—the essence of worship for us. And because we valued heart expression, we sometimes tried different things to stretch us and allow for something new to be expressed. As I was explaining this to those who might be the most uncomfortable (although in my experience, the more unchurched you are the more you actually like this stuff!), I was also restating to our church community our values in the area of worship, reminding them that we actually believe in stepping out creatively and exploring the use of the arts. This experience became a teachable moment. Far from being a failure, it became just another step on our journey together.

People in the congregation began to relax. The most on-edge people in the room, however, were the members of the worship team. I turned to them and thanked them for their courage to take a risk. This put them in shock, as they had been expecting to be escorted from the stage, never to be heard from again! I explained to the church what a vulnerable position worship leading is and how much support this team (and all the other teams) needed from us. I encouraged everyone to stretch out their hands toward the worship team (with appropriate explanation to those unfamiliar with our culture) and to pray for and encourage the artists on the stage.

Before long, tears began to flow, and one of the most tangible experiences of community I had ever felt began to fill the room. I then turned to the team and asked them to continue to lead us in worship. They were still in shock. Instead of being given the boot, they were being prayed for and asked to continue. *Now* it was no longer about the songs and the style and the presentation as much as it was about community. Soon we launched into one of the best of times of corporate worship I can remember. It was a watershed moment for our church and for my growing understanding of worship.

I *know* that God was listening.

Take the Journey into Justice

The simplest principle I can state about justice interwoven in worship is to not assume that the marginalized, the poor and the broken of our culture and society are a distraction. Sometimes, they are the very point of worship. But we must find ways to allow them access and to move them from being an outreach or a charity to becoming part of the identity of the church.

We must also make room for the silenced and muted voices around us to find their expression. This is a challenge, and it is necessary to equip the community in order to understand it, but the rewards are outstanding. These voices, depending on the setting, can be anyone—from the youth to an ethnic group that has not yet been given a way to influence the worshipful expression of the whole body.

I am not talking about "special music" or a presentation every once in a while, although that may be a good place to start. I am not just talking about translating songs or interpreting preaching for another language, although that may be helpful. I am inviting you to wrestle with how to weave the marginalized into the very fabric of your expression of worship and give them their own voice in the midst of corporate community.

In one of the churches my wife and I planted, we were situated in an area that had a high population of First Nations people. In the States they are known as Native Americans. Over the years, we wrote songs that used some of the aboriginal languages and introduced rhythms and dance that these people led us in, dressed in their regalia. These were some of the sweetest times in God's presence that I can recall. We didn't do it often, and it wasn't as if the rest of us who were white were trying to be Native; this was about community and honor. The nearness of the Lord became tangible, and I am sure that He was listening and participating in our worship.

COMMUNICATION FIRST

To move ahead in any of these aspects of the journey of worship, communication is key. It entails close partnering between those who carry governmental oversight for the church and those who carry responsibility for the worship expression. Many times, this is the place where the breakdowns occur.

I am in a unique position as both a governmental leader in the church community and as someone who is known for worship leading. I go to all the meetings. I'll sit in the pastor's conference, and sure enough, before long the topic of wacky worship leaders and the artists comes up. Then I'll sit in the worship conference, and sure enough, before long the topic of the controlling and insensitive pastor is discussed.

We must move beyond this impasse if we are to move forward into the worship God is seeking. It is a journey we take together. Keeping in step with the desires of God in regard to worship will stretch any community of Christ's followers. But this is at the heart of our mandate. This is who we are. To fall short here is to lose everything.

So, there *is* a worship that God is looking for. To embark on the journey of its discovery is to pursue the path of the Church's highest calling. If we dare to take this seriously, we must be prepared for anything. This is a path of unpredictability and change. It would seem that to worship an idol would be much easier—at least we know where it is all times, and the protocol is set in place. But we have encountered the Living God of heaven. Our whole lives are caught up in His advancing Kingdom and the worship at its center. In reverence and awe, let us continue to take steps forward in the eternal pursuit of the worship God is seeking.

But you have come to Mount Zion, to the heavenly Jerusalem, the city of the living God. You have come to thousands upon thousands of angels in joyful assembly, to the church of the firstborn, whose names are written in heaven. You have come to God, the judge of all [people], to the spirits of righteous [people] made perfect, to Jesus the mediator of a new covenant, and to the sprinkled blood that speaks a better word than the blood of Abel.

See to it that you do not refuse him who speaks. If they did not escape when they refused him who warned them on earth, how much less will we, if we turn away from him who warns us from heaven? At that time his voice shook the earth, but now he has promised, "Once more I will shake not only the earth but also the heavens." The words "once more" indicate the removing of what can be shaken—that is, created things—so that what cannot be shaken may remain.Therefore, since we are receiving a kingdom that cannot be shaken, let us be thankful, and so worship God acceptably with reverence and awe, for our God is a consuming fire.

HEBREWS 12:22-29

EndNOTES

Chapter One

1. Don Williams, *Signs and Wonders and the Kingdom of God* (Ann Arbor, MI: Vine Books, 1989), p. 42.

2. Matthew Henry, *Commentary on the Whole Bible: Genesis to Revelation*, Psalms 22:1-10, ed. Leslie F. Church (Grand Rapids, MI: Zondervan Publishing House, 1961,) p. 12.

3. John Wimber, *Power Healing* (San Francisco: HarperSan Francisco, 1987), pp. 174-175.

4. A. W. Tozer, *Worship: The Missing Jewel* (Camp Hill, PA: Christian Publications, 1992), n.p.

Chapter Two

1. C. H. Spurgeon, *The Treasury of David*, vol. 2: Psalm LVIII to LXXXVII (McLean, VA: MacDonald Publishing Company), p. 477.

2. J. B. Payne, *The Zondervan Pictorial Encyclopedia of the Bible*, vol. 5: Q-Z (Grand Rapids, MI: Zondervan Publishing House 1975, 1976), p. 1066.

3. N. T. Wright, *For All God's Worth: True Worship and the Calling of the Church* (Grand Rapids, MI: Eerdmans Publishing Company, 1997), p. 57.

4. Spurgeon, *The Treasury of David*, p. 478.

5. Payne, Pictorial Encyclopedia, n.p.

6. It is totally appropriate to equate the "register of the peoples" in Psalm 87 with the book of life referred to in the book of Revelation. Isaiah also points to this reality in Isaiah 4:3.

Chapter Three

1. H. R. Rookmaaker, *The Creative Gift—Essays on Art and the Christian Life* (Westchester, IL: Cornerstone Books, 1981), p. 71.

2. Richard Tarnas, *The Passion of the Western Mind* (New York: Ballantine Books, 1991), p. 396.

3. A. W. Tozer, *A Treasury of A. W. Tozer* (Harrisburg, PA: Christian Publications, 1980), p. 40.

4. Francis Foulkes, *The Epistle of Paul to the Ephesians*, Tyndale New Testament Commentaries (Grand Rapids, MI: Eerdmans Publishing Company, 1981), p. 60.

Chapter Four

1. *Vine's Expository Dictionary of Biblical Words* (Nashville, TN: Thomas Nelson Publishers, 1985), s.v. "zeteo." Quoted in *PC Study Bible* CD-ROM. Biblesoft, 1994.

2. Don Williams, *Signs and Wonders and the Kingdom* (Ann Arbor, MI: Vine Books, 1989), p. 38.

3. *Vine's Expository Dictionary of Biblical Words*, s.v. "pater."

4. *Vine's Expository Dictionary of Biblical Words*, s.v. "pneuma."

5. *Vine's Expository Dictionary of Biblical Words*, s.v. "alethia."

6. Matt Redman, *The Unquenchable Worshipper* (Ventura, CA: Regal Books, 2001), p. 65.

Chapter Five

1. L. Berkhof, *Systematic Theology* (Grand Rapids, MI: Eerdmans Publishing Company, 1941), p. 126; see also Revelation 4:11.
2. John Piper, *The Pleasures of God: Meditations on God's Delight in Being God* (Portland, OR: Multnomah Press, 1991), p. 84.
3. Franky Schaeffer, *Addicted to Mediocrity*, (Westchester, IL: Crossway Books, 1981), pp. 23-24.

Chapter Six

1. N. T. Wright, *For All God's Worth: True Worship and the Calling of the Church* (Grand Rapids, MI: Eerdmans Publishing Company, 1997), p. 47.
2. Arthur F. Glasser; with Charles Van Egen, Dean S. Gilliland, and Shawn B. Redford; *Announcing the Kingdom: The Story of God's Mission in the Bible* (Grand Rapids, MI: Baker Academic, 2003), p. 340.
3. Wright, *For All God's Worth*, p. 48.
4. "The Life and Times of Georg Friedrich Handel," *Devine Entertainment Corporation*. http://www.devine-ent.com/shows/composers/handel-bio.shtml, emphasis added (accessed June 2004).
5. This edition of *Glimpses* is abridged and adapted from a chapter on Handel in Patrick Cavanaugh, *The Spiritual Lives of the Great Composers* (Nashville, TN: Sparrow Press, 1992).
6. *Vine's Expository Dictionary of Biblical Words*, s.v. "tepillah."
7. Glasser, *Announcing the Kingdom,* pp. 337-338.

8. I. H. Marshall, "Salvation," *New Dictionary of Theology*, ed. Sinclair B. Ferguson, David F. Wright, and J. I. Packer (Downers Grove, IL: InterVarsity Press, 1988), p. 611.

9. Ibid., p. 591, emphasis added.

10. Glasser, *Announcing the Kingdom,* p. 339.

11. *New Dictionary of Theology*, p. 592.

12. David Moberg, *The Great Reversal: Evangelism Versus Social Concern* (New York: J.B. Lippincott Company, 1972), n.p.

Chapter Seven

1. Based on Matthew 26:6-13; Mark 14:3-9; John 12:1-8; W. T. Dayton, "Mary of Bethany," *The Zondervan Pictorial Encyclopedia of the Bible*, vol. 4 (Grand Rapids, MI: Zondervan Publishers, 1980), p. 104; William Hendriksen, *New Testament Commentary, The Gospel of Matthew* (Grand Rapids, MI: Baker Book House, 1973), pp. 898-901.

2. Hendriksen, *New Testament Commentary*, p. 899.

3. Matthew Henry, *Commentary on the Whole Bible: Genesis to Revelation,* Matthew 26, ed. Leslie F. Church (Grand Rapids, MI: Zondervan Publishing House, 1961), n.p.

4. Ibid.